SPIRIT, SOUL, AND BODY(II)

Dr. Jaerock Lee

The Story of the Spiritual World Unfolded in Space!

SPIRIT, SOUL, AND BODY(II)

Dr. Jaerock Lee

URIM BOOKS

Spirit, Soul, and Body (II) by Dr. Jaerock Lee
Published by Urim Books (Representative: Seongkeon Vin)
361-66, Shindaebang-Dong, Dongjak-Gu, Seoul, Korea
www.urimbooks.com

First Published March 2013

Previously published into Korean by Urim Books in 2010

Edited by Dr. Geumsun Vin
Designed by Editorial Bureau of Urim Books
Printed by Yewon Printing Company
For more information contact: urimbook@hotmail.com

Foreword

From the time I accepted Jesus Christ and began to read the Bible, I began to pray to deeply understand the heart of God. God answered me after seven years of countless prayers and periods of fasting. After I opened a church, God explained to me many difficult passages in the Bible through the inspiration of the Holy Spirit, just one of which is the detailed contents concerning 'Spirit, Soul, and Body'. This is the mysterious story that lets us understand the origin of men and allows us to understand ourselves. It is the account of what I had not been able to hear anywhere else, and it is my joy that is great beyond description.

When I delivered these messages on spirit, soul, and body, there were many testimonies and responses both from within Korea and overseas. Many say they realized themselves, understood what kinds of beings they were, and received answers to many difficult passages in the Bible as well as understanding the ways to gain true life. Some of those people say they now have the goal to become a person of spirit and participate in the divine nature of God and they strive to achieve it as recorded in 2 Peter 1:4, which reads, *"For by these He has granted to us His precious and magnificent promises, so that by them you may become partakers of the divine nature, having escaped the corruption that is in the world by lust."*

Sun Tzu's *The Art of War* says that if you know yourself and your enemy, you will never lose any battle. The messages on "Spirit, Soul, and Body" shed light on the deep part of our 'self' and they teach us about the origin of men. Once we learn and understand this message thoroughly, we will also be able to understand any kind of person. We will also learn the ways to defeat the forces of darkness, which have been affecting us, so that we can lead victorious Christian lives.

Volume 2 of Spirit, Soul, and Body in particular will explain about the origin of the Creator God, the vast spiritual space, and the space of light where our spirit will dwell. There are some full-color pictures to help you better understand the form of God and space. Once we understand the secrets of the spaces and become a person of whole spirit, we can go beyond the human limitations to use the space of God, and we can even see the form of God. That is why Jesus said in John 14:12, *"Truly, truly, I say to you, he who believes in Me, the works that I do, he will do also; and greater works than these he will do; because I go to the Father."*

I would like to give thanks to the director Geumsun Vin and all the staff of the editorial bureau. I hope that through this book, the readers will have the qualifications to enter into the space of light and experience the wondrous spaces of God.

March 2010,

Jaerock Lee

Beginning the Second Journey of Spirit, Soul, and Body

"Now may the God of peace Himself sanctify you entirely; and may your spirit and soul and body be preserved complete, without blame at the coming of our Lord Jesus Christ" (1 Thessalonians 5:23).

Today, cyber space is open to anybody who has access to the Internet, but people make use of it to different degrees according to the extent of the knowledge of computers and Internet-related skills they have. Likewise, to the extent that we understand the space of God, we can understand the amazing miracles in the Bible and experience such works of God in our daily lives.

The Bible tells us many events from which we can understand the spaces of God. When Stephen was being martyred by stoning, the gate of Heaven opened and he saw the Son of Man standing on the right hand of God (Acts 7:56). This was made possible because God opened the space of the fourth heaven. Peter was imprisoned while preaching the gospel, but was released by the help of angels. The apostle Paul had a similar experience when he was put in jail in Philippi. God opened the space of the third heaven to send a mighty angel who loosened the chains and opened the gates.

Once we cultivate the heart of whole spirit, we will be

able to use the space of God on this earth and nothing will be impossible. Furthermore, we will enjoy eternal life and blessings in New Jerusalem in the future. On the other hand, for a person who has not come into whole spirit yet, he/she needs to fulfill the measure of justice to be able to make use of God's space. This book is full of the stories that are spread out in the limitless space of spirit.

This book helps the readers to do the following:

1. It helps them understand the love of God who divided the spaces, dimensions, and light and darkness in His providence of human cultivation to gain true children. When we accept Jesus Christ and act with faith, we can enjoy the right as the children of light and go into the beautiful space of light.

2. Heaven is in the space of light. It is categorized into many dwelling places from Paradise to New Jerusalem. We will live there in Heaven in perfected heavenly bodies. We will enjoy the eternal life in Heaven which is filled with happiness and joy, and this is God's gift for us.

3. It is the power of God alone that can make us true children of God who have the image of God. Through the power of God, we can go into the beautiful space of light and also experience wondrous and powerful works beyond human limitations on this earth.

CONTENTS

CONTENTS

Part 1

Vast Space
of the Spiritual Realm

What Happened in Heaven Before the Creation?
How Were the Space of Light and Space of Darkness Formed?

> *"This is the message we have heard from Him*
> *and announce to you, that God is Light,*
> *and in Him there is no darkness at all."*
> - 1 John 1:5

> *"To Him who rides upon the highest heavens,*
> *which are from ancient times; Behold,*
> *He speaks forth with His voice,*
> *a mighty voice."*
> - Psalm 68:33

Chapter 1
Darkness and Light

There are light and darkness not only in this visible world,
but there are spaces of light and darkness in the spiritual world as well.
What is the reason that God allowed for the space of darkness to exist
and who is the ruler of darkness?

Vast Spiritual Space and the Original God

God Planned Human Cultivation

The Original God Became the Trinity

God Created Angels and Cherubim

The Failed Rebellion of Lucifer

God's Providence in Dividing Light and Darkness

When you were a child did you ever fall asleep while counting the number of stars in the sky? I believe many of you have such a memory. There are so many stars that can be seen with our eyes, but there are innumerably more stars that are not seen. How big is this universe?

Even with the development of science, men have not been able to calculate the exact size of the universe. It's because it is an endlessly vast space. The planets like the Earth gather to form a solar system, and many solar systems and other heavenly bodies gather together to form a galaxy. Multiple numbers of galaxies again form a group of galaxies, and groups of galaxies form microcosmos and microcosmoses make up the great universe.

The size of our solar system in our galaxy is seen only as a tiny dot. This galaxy is also like a mere dot compared to the size of the whole universe. This physical universe alone cannot be measured with the most sophisticated scientific equipment. But, compared with the spiritual space, it too is only a very small portion.

In addition to this physical universe that we see, there is a spiritual space that stretches endlessly in another dimension. The Bible mentions multiple numbers of 'heavens'.

Deuteronomy 10:14 reads, *"Behold, to the LORD your God belong heaven and the highest heavens, the earth and all that is in it,"* and Nehemiah 9:6 reads, *"You alone are the LORD. You have made the heavens, the heaven of heavens with all their host, the earth and all that is on it, the seas and all that is in them. You give life to all of them and the heavenly host bows down before You."*

How did many heavens come to exist, and what happened in these heavens before the creation of this world? Let us go back to the time before the creation of this world. It was before the universe and galaxy that we know existed. The universe back then was not the same universe as our universe now. It was just one huge space without the distinction between the spiritual space and the physical space.

Vast Spiritual Space and the Original God

The vast spiritual space refers to the original universe as a whole. It was this space that the original God harbored before the ages. Here, 'original God' refers to God, who existed as light and voice before the creation. The original universe refers to the universe where the original God existed alone.

What was the original appearance of God? Imagine beautiful lights filling up the endlessly vast universe, and those lights were swelling and rolling like waves. As 1 John 1:5 says, *"God is Light,"* God stretched out all throughout the original universe in the form of such beautiful and brilliant lights.

The 'auroras' help us understand this form of the original God. Auroras are seen in the skies near the Polar Regions. They usually have beautiful red, blue, yellow, light green, or pink colors. It is said aurora lights are so beautiful that those who have seen them can never forget the beauty.

Romans 1:20 says, *"For since the creation of the world His invisible attributes, His eternal power and divine nature, have been clearly seen, being understood through what has been made, so that they are without excuse."* God has created such lights as the auroras so that we are able to understand God's original appearance when we wonder about the original God.

The original God had a clear and pure yet majestic voice in the lights that rolled like waves. Have you heard the whisper-like sounds that accompany a gentle breeze? In the wind coming from the sea, you can hear the gentle sound of the waves. Similar to the way sound is carried within the winds, the voice chimed out from the original light itself. As sound is carried by the wind, the original voice spread together with the original lights throughout the whole universe while embracing it at the same time.

However, if you hear the voice of God even just once, you will never be able to forget that voice. I heard it a couple of times, and it was so majestic, pure, and clean. It means it is so grand and pure. The voice of God is in fact very clear and pure, sweet, and yet so majestic that it is able to ring throughout the entire universe.

John 1:1 says, *"In the beginning was the Word, and the Word was with God, and the Word was God."* This Word that was in the beginning is the original voice that was chiming from within the original light. The above verse expressed God as 'Word' which is the essence, rather than the form of God, which is the light. The 'Word' is the content, and 'God' is the name given to the content. So, the essence of God is 'Word', and His existence was in the form of lights and voice that filled the whole universe.

God Planned Human Cultivation

At a certain point in the limitless timeline, God who existed alone planned 'human cultivation':

'What if there were a being who could know about this vast universe and My heart, and share love with Me? What if he could understand and receive My heart and emotions that I share with him and he could give his heart to Me in return? What a happy and joyful thing it would be!'

God wanted another being with whom He could communicate and share everything in the universe. In particular, God wanted a being with whom He could share His love. God made the plan of 'human cultivation' with a desire to start a new work to gain His true children.

What do you think God did first in the plan for human cultivation? God formerly existed as light that was spread all throughout the whole universe, but He coalesced at the peak of the spiritual realm and came to have a form of light. As He cohered as one light, different dimensions of the 'heavens' were made. Here, 'heaven' is synonymous with the space in the universe. At first, there was only one original universe, but as the original God coalesced and cohered as one light, different spaces in universe were made. It's because as the lights that were spread throughout the universe came together and concentrated at the peak of the spiritual realm, different spaces were made according to the brightness of the light.

In the past, the brightness of the light was the same everywhere in the original universe, but now, the peak of the spiritual realm became the brightest. For example, if you put 10,000 lights evenly in a hall, the brightness will be the same everywhere in the hall. But what would happen if you put one light, of which the brightness is the same as that of 10,000 lights, at the center of the hall? The closer to the central area, the brighter the light would be, and the inverse is true as that distance increases. Similarly, when the original light became one condensed light, different spaces were created according to the differences in the brightness in the space.

The original light is a spiritual light, and as the brightness of the light changed, the density of the spiritual nature also changed. When the original light came together as one condensed light, the brightness of the light and the density of spirit became less dense as distance from the source increased. So, the original universe that used to exist as one space was categorized into four different universes according to the brightness of the light and the density of spirit. God called them the first, second, third, and fourth heavens.

The place where God the Origin cohered as the one light is a very special place that belongs to the fourth heaven. Therefore, the light is the brightest in the fourth heaven, and so is the density of the spirit. The third heaven has less brightness of light and density of spirit than those of the fourth heaven, and so is the case with the second heaven. The spiritual realm consists of the second to the fourth heavens. The first heaven is the physical universe that we see with our eyes. This is a universe where the nature of spirit was almost completely taken away when God coalesced as one light, and thus it is filled with the nature of flesh instead of spirit.

In the physical space, if you cut a certain space into four parts, each space is smaller than the original one. But it is not the case with the spiritual space. It is because there are no limits in the spiritual space. When the vast limitless universe divided into four, it was four vast limitless universes. Therefore, even though the original universe divided into four heavens, there is no limit to each heaven. Not only the Second, Third, and Fourth Heavens, but the First Heaven which is a fleshly world also doesn't have limit.

God let there be these different heavens according to the usage. First, God separated the First Heaven to set it as the stage for the human cultivation. The Second Heaven was prepared as a space for the spirits of darkness which are necessary for the human cultivation. But it was also for Adam who was created as a living spirit. The Third Heaven was separated to build the heavenly kingdom where the good wheat that would be gained through human cultivation would enter. Finally, the Fourth Heaven is the space for God the Trinity. It is in the same dimension as the universe that used to be one original space.

When the original universe was first separated into four heavens, those heavens were not filled with any contents. But it does not mean they were completely empty. There were countless stars in the original universe. In the First Heaven, our Earth, solar system, and our galaxy had not been made yet. In the Third Heaven, the kingdom of heaven had not yet been made. It was just a suitable space to make the heavenly kingdom. After this separation of spaces, God began to fill these spaces with His works of creation.

The Original God Became the Trinity

After cohering as one light, God first separated Himself into three lights. Here, when saying that 'a light divides into three lights,' the idea is not like that a certain lump is divided into three pieces. It is rather like two more identical lights are issued forth from within the original one light. Even though the original light separated into three, these three are not separate or different, but they are the same as the original.

The original light had existed as one, and the other two lights were newly made. After becoming three lights, the lights put on a spiritual form that is like that of a man. They came to exist as God the Father, God the Son, and God the Holy Spirit. After God the Origin divided into God the Trinity, each one of the Trinity put on their own spiritual body, which is a little different from each other. But the spirits inside the spiritual bodies came forth from the same original God, so one might say that the Three in One all have the same heart, thoughts, power, and wisdom.

That is why we refer to God the Father, God the Son, and God the Holy Spirit as the Trinity. God the Trinity first created the things that were necessary for the space where God dwelled. When God existed alone as light and voice permeated within it, He did not need a dwelling place. But because He now had a form, He needed a place to dwell.

When God the Trinity stays in the Fourth Heaven, He may or may not put on a form. He can change His form as He wants in the Fourth Heaven, and because He sometimes wears a form, there is a dwelling place in there. God always has a form in the Third Heaven that also accommodates the kingdom of heaven, and thus He created a dwelling place for Himself there. God also began to create spiritual beings that would minister to Him.

God Created Angels and Cherubim

There are two kinds of spiritual beings that God created;

they are 'angels' and 'cherubim.' An angel is almost the same in its form as that of a man except that it has wings (Revelation 14:6). Men were created in the image of God, and so were the angels (Mark 16:5). It's just that angels only have the outer image of God while men have the outer image as well as the heart of God.

What about the size of the angels? There are angels that are similar to men. However, there are very tiny angels and huge angels as well. They have the form and characteristics according to their roles.

For example, if there is an angel who plays the role of an army general, an angel of masculine form would be more appropriate. For dancing and singing, feminine angels would be more appropriate. Of course, it doesn't mean that there are no masculine angels that dance. Just as there are male dancers in this world and they play their roles, there are male-like angels as well. But, their existence as masculine or feminine angels in appearance or character does not mean they have gender. It just means that their appearances and behaviors are perceived like a male or female.

Angels serve God and fulfill their duties by the order of God. There are many kinds of duties, and there are countless numbers of angels.

And all the angels were standing around the throne and around the elders and the four living creatures; and

11

they fell on their faces before the throne and worshiped God (Revelation 7:11).

I saw another strong angel coming down out of heaven, clothed with a cloud; and the rainbow was upon his head, and his face was like the sun, and his feet like pillars of fire (Revelation 10:1).

Are they not all ministering spirits, sent out to render service for the sake of those who will inherit salvation? (Hebrews 1:14).

Among them, while there are angels that are given a unique duty in the spiritual realm, there are other angels that minister to the children of God on earth. The number of angels assigned to each believer will differ according to the extent to which each person is sanctified to have become men of spirit or whole spirit. The hierarchy among the angels is set and kept strictly according to the spiritual hierarchy of their masters. Also, there are angels that are assigned to each individual person whether he is a believer or not. They are the angels that record every single word and deed of each person who is living on this earth.

While angels have the image of men, the cherubim have forms like those of various animals. Those cherubim that have the duty of escorting God have the shapes of different animals such as lion, eagle, and cow or ox. Psalm 18:10 reads, *"He rode upon a cherub and flew; and He sped upon the wings of the wind."*

Dragons, which people think are an imaginary animal, in fact used to be one of the cherubim. The dragon that God first created was so beautiful and lovely, and it was like a pet animal for God. It had soft fur and hands and feet, and its various beautiful colors were beautiful beyond description. Dragons were the head of the cherubim and had a great deal of power and authority. They had a vast number of messengers under their control.

Among the cherubim are the 'four living creatures'. They look like a solid mass of steel with a dark color. The four living creatures bring about disasters and punishments by the command of God. They show the dignity and authority of God. They have one head, but four faces which are faces of a man, a lion, a calf, and an eagle. They appear as if four persons were standing with their backs facing toward the inside and their faces facing outward. In the center space is a flame that goes up and down. Their whole body is filled with eyes and they watch everything.

When God created angels and the cherubim, He did not give them the freewill that was given men. They would just obey God's command given according to the hierarchy. Even today God rules over the whole universe through these angels and cherubim.

Spiritual Realm Is Well-Organized and Systematized.

The Bible also mentions about heavenly host and archangels. Luke 2:13 says, *"And suddenly there appeared with the angel a multitude of the heavenly host praising God ..."* Heavenly host is the heavenly army.

Also, 1 Thessalonians 4:16 says, *"For the Lord Himself will descend from heaven with a shout, with the voice of the archangel and with the trumpet of God, and the dead in Christ will rise first."* The fact that there are archangels tells us that there are orders in the world of angels.

The archangels search every aspect acting like the hands and feet and eyes and ears of God. They also receive commands and make reports to God directly. Under these archangels that are like ministers, there are countless angels supporting them. These archangels do not direct all the angels under them; they have other head angels to manage a certain unit of angels. In this system, once a command is given, it is delivered correctly, and all reports are perfectly error-free. Though there are many steps, this process is carried out instantly.

God can rule over and search every person on this earth while on His throne thanks to the roles of the angels. Of course, God is almighty and He can search everything on His own. Nevertheless, the angels report to God what they see and check directly. In this way, the angels will be not only reporters but also witnesses to their reports. This adds more light of justice on the judgment of God, when He judges something.

For example, we can talk about the punishment inflicted upon Sodom and Gomorrah. Genesis 19:1 says, *"Now the two angels came to Sodom in the evening."* God sent His angels to search once again before He punished Sodom and Gomorrah. And the people there showed such rebellious acts. That is, they tried to harm even these angels. Eventually, God punished Sodom and Gomorrah with fire.

Some of the most well-known archangels are Gabriel and Michael. Gabriel is a messenger that appears to deliver special revelation or words of God. He is big and dignified, and wears a robe with big sleeves, which can contain the revelation of God. Just as a minister who delivers the order of the king has a symbol, Gabriel also wears a robe that has the pattern which is like the royal seal.

The archangel Michael is like the chief of the army, and he has dignity in his eyes. He wears an armored suit, a belt around his waist that can hold many kinds of weapons inside. Having weapons in spiritual realm means that God has given him the authority to fight spiritual battles. Different kinds of symbolic weapons would be drawn according to how fierce the battle is.

There are also two huge archangels. They have feminine images and great power and authority. They don't usually smile. If they appear, God's great works are accompanied with them. They are so tall that even if they stand in a building with a high ceiling, you can just see the edge of their robes. We cannot measure how tall they could be, for the spiritual realm has a completely different concept of measurement than the physical world.

Three Archangels That Belong to God Directly

In addition to those many angels, God created some angels under His direct control that would minister to Him personally. They were the three archangels including Lucifer. They had the position and dignity like other archangels, but they had very special authority.

Generally speaking, spiritual beings were not given freewill. They were only able to unconditionally obey God. But for those three archangels that belong to God directly, by exception God gave them humanity and freewill, which only human beings can have. God created them to have humanity and to share love with Him although they cannot exactly be like God's children who are gained through human cultivation. God allowed for them to serve Him with their heart and share the feelings of joy and happiness with Him with their freewill.

The three archangels had feminine appearances, and they had gentle, meek, and good heart. The words that came out of their mouths were filled with good aroma, and their behaviors were elegant. But each of them had a little bit of difference in their characters. Lucifer had more of the strong characters than the other two. Lucifer was in charge of music, and she pleased God with beautiful voice and musical instruments. God was very delighted with her praising and loved her very much.

Once, God showed me Lucifer. She was wearing a big and splendid dress that was decorated with precious gemstones. Her hair was adorned with jewels hanging down which were in perfect harmony with her blonde hair. She was playing a magnificent musical instrument. The chiming sound of the gemstones and the sound of praise mingled together and spread out like the wind would blow. The sound went up to God and it was so beautiful.

But as she was loved very much by God and enjoyed great power for a long time, arrogance began to grow in her mind. As she saw all the things that God was doing and His great authority to rule over the whole spiritual realm, she envied it. Arrogance grew in her mind that she thought she would be able to do better than God. Finally, she made a plan to lift herself higher than God and began to gather her forces.

Lucifer had such great power that she first began to gather the angels under her authority at her side. Along with countless angels, she also enticed the dragons and many of the cherubim under their control. She allured them by pretending that she was doing a secret mission for God.

The Failed Rebellion of Lucifer

God knew Lucifer's mind and gave her a chance to turn back. He let her know about the consequences of the rebellion in an attempt to let her look straight at the reality. But, arrogance already settled in Lucifer's mind, and she did not turn away.

Lucifer rebelled against God and was defeated. She was driven out along with the spiritual beings that followed her and was confined in the Abyss, or otherwise known as the 'bottomless pit'.

Isaiah 14:12-15 explains about the rebellion and defeat of Lucifer and the final result:

> How you have fallen from heaven, O star of the morning, son of the dawn! You have been cut down to the earth, you who have weakened the nations! But you said in your heart, "I will ascend to heaven; I will raise my throne above the stars of God, and I will sit on the mount of assembly in the recesses of the north. I will ascend above the heights of the clouds; I will make myself like the Most High." Nevertheless you will be thrust down to Sheol, to the recesses of the pit.

The Bible also writes about the angels that followed Lucifer. 2 Peter 2:4 says, "For if God did not spare angels when they sinned, but cast them into hell and committed them to pits of darkness, reserved for judgment..." Jude 1:6 also says, "And angels who did not keep their own domain, but abandoned their proper abode, He has kept in eternal bonds under darkness for the judgment of the great day..."

Genesis 1:2 also talks about what happened in the spiritual realm before the creation of this world. It says, "The earth was formless and void, and darkness was over the surface of the *deep, and the Spirit of God was moving over the surface of the waters."*

This verse has both spiritual and physical meanings. It implies what had happened in the spiritual realm as well as the things that were taking place in the physical world.

Spiritually, saying "the earth was formless" signifies that the spiritual order was momentarily disturbed due to the rebellion of Lucifer. The 'earth' symbolizes 'the world of darkness controlled by Lucifer'. Because Lucifer and the beings that followed her broke the order set by God, it is said that the earth was formless. Next, it says the earth was 'void'. This expresses the heart of God after He was betrayed by Lucifer whom He had loved so much.

But the rebellion was soon repressed and the evil spirits were confined in the deepest part of Hell, the Abyss. This is expressed in the phrase, "darkness was over the surface of the deep." God brought order and peace back by putting the power of darkness in the Abyss, and this is explained in the phrase, "the Spirit of God was moving over the surface of the waters."

God Created Earth in the First Heaven

When the Earth was first made, the condition was not like today. There was seismic activity, volcano eruptions, and movements of the Earth's plates and crust. There were also many kinds of activities taking place in the atmosphere.

Thus, this unstable condition of the Earth is explained in the phrase, "...the earth was formless and void." Next the verse says,

19

"...darkness was over the surface of the deep." It means that when the Earth was first created, there was no sun, moon, or any other stars in our galaxy, and thus the Earth was covered by darkness. When God was filling the Earth with the necessary things, He expended all His best efforts. Just like a father who is building and filling the house for his family with all his care, He harbored the whole Earth and accomplished His work of creation.

This process is explained in the expression, "the Spirit of God was moving over the surface of the waters." At this time, God Himself came down to this Earth. He searched for what the Earth would need and how He would make those things, going all over the Earth. The Bible says the Spirit of God was moving over the 'surface of waters'. It tells us that the Earth at that time was covered by water completely. Just like a fetus grows up in the amniotic fluid in the uterus, the Earth was covered by waters for a very long time until before the six-day creation took place on the Earth.

Then, where did this water come from that covered whole Earth? This water was the water of life that flowed out from the throne of God. God made the water of life when He created the vast spiritual realm, and He brought this water to the Earth. The reason why He covered this Earth with the water of life was to make a good environment for all the living things including human beings to live on this Earth in the future.

We cannot find any other planet that is so full of water like the Earth in the solar system. In fact, we have not found any other planet that has enough water to support life anywhere. It is because God brought this water of life only to the Earth and made the basic environment where living things would be able to continue their lives.

When God covered the Earth with the water of life, He wanted all men to gain eternal life in God. He wanted all human beings who would live on the Earth to come forth as true children who have pure and clean hearts like the water of life.

God's Providence in Dividing Light and Darkness

Finally, God began His first day of creation. Genesis 1:3-4 says, *"Then God said, 'Let there be light'; and there was light. God saw that the light was good; and God separated the light from the darkness."* God said, "Let there be light." The light here is spiritual light and it is the light that flows out from the throne of God. It has the power and divinity of God. God covered the Earth with this light and established the foundation of the Earth so that it would not be formless and void but it would be operated in an orderly and systematic manner.

Then, Genesis 1:4-5 says, *"God saw that the light was good; and God separated the light from the darkness. God called the light day, and the darkness He called night. And there was evening and there was morning, one day."* By commanding for the light to exist, the basic order and rules of nature were established on the Earth, and thus, even when there was no sun or moon, it was being operated as if there were the sun and the

21

moon. In other words, the day and the night on the Earth were not made by the sun and the moon. The order and rule regarding the day and the night had been already established by God, and the sun and the moon were later created to govern the day and the night.

But separating the day and the night has a more important spiritual meaning than the physical separation. It means that on the first day of the creation God released Lucifer and some of the fallen angels from the Abyss and the realm of evil spirits was formed. God knew that there needed to be spiritual light and darkness for human cultivation just as everything on the Earth runs by the cycle of day and night. He planned everything even before the ages, and when the time came, He gave the authority to Lucifer, who had betrayed God, to make her the ruler of darkness.

But it does not mean that He gave her the same authority as the authority of God who is the Master and Owner of the vast universe. He allowed for her spiritual beings and the order and system of the world of evil spirits exclusively for the purpose of human cultivation, so that human cultivation would be carried out fairly and within justice. Actually, Lucifer the ruler of darkness used to belong to the light but she came out of it and became corrupted. She still falls under the ultimate power and authority of God.

God Allowed for the Space of Darkness in the Second Heaven

Genesis 1:6-8 says, *"Then God said, 'Let there be an expanse in the midst of the waters, and let it separate the waters from the waters.' God made the expanse, and separated the waters which were below the expanse from the waters which were above the expanse; and it was so. God called the expanse heaven. And there was evening and there was morning, a second day."*

With the water of life that flowed out from the throne of God, God stabilized the Earth which was to be the stage for human cultivation. Then He created the expanse. The expanse that was on Earth refers to the atmosphere that was made. God then separated the water that covered the Earth into the water below the expanse and one above the expanse.

The water below the expanse is the water that remained on Earth. On the third day of the creation, the waters gathered at one place to form the ocean, and it became the source to form other bodies of water such as rivers and lakes on Earth. The water above the expanse was used for meteorological phenomena such as cloud formation and precipitation, but the main use of this water was for the Garden of Eden.

When the Bible says 'expanse' it does not only refer to the sky that we see. In Genesis 1, it says everything God created during the six days of creation was 'good', that is except for the second day. On the second day God did not pronounce it as 'good'. The reason is that on the second day God allowed for the space of darkness to be formed in the second heaven for the evil spirits, for they were be given the 'power of the air' and later used as instruments in the process of human cultivation.

Ephesians 2:2 says, *"...in which you formerly walked according to the course of this world, according to the prince of the power of the air, of the spirit that is now working in the sons of disobedience."* This tells us that the space of darkness where the evil spirits dwell is the 'air'. It is the space that is adjacent to and east of the Garden of Eden. This is where the evil spirits will dwell until human cultivation is finished.

Of course, the Garden of Eden is also in the second heaven as well as the space for the Seven-year Wedding Banquet that will be held after the human cultivation is done. But, because the space of darkness where the evil spirits would have power was formed, God did not say it was 'good' on the second day.

The World of Evil Spirits

Before she became the ruler of darkness, Lucifer had seen and learned many things being so close to God the Father. She saw how God ruled over the vast spiritual space through the angels and cherubim, and when she formed the world of evil spirits, she imitated the ways of God. She established two chains of command to pass orders and govern the world of darkness. One is the command chain of the dragons and their angels and the other is the chain of Satan and devils.

First, Lucifer gave the dragons practical authority similar to that of army generals and organized the angels under their charge to support their works. The four dragons that have the 'power of the air' control the men of darkness in order to receive their worship. The dragons penetrate into the places of idolatry which results in the people worshipping them.

Lucifer controls everything 'behind the scenes' while working through Satan. Satan controls men's thoughts of untruth having exactly the same heart and thoughts of Lucifer. Satan does not have a solid form, and it appears as dark smoke. For this reason those who receive the works of Satan have something like a dark cloud around their face. For some people, the dark smoke covers their whole body from head to foot.

And it is the work of the devil that incites the people to put the thoughts of untruth into action. Some of the fallen angels were released and are acting as devils. The devil does the opposite things of angels, wearing completely black attire.

When a person does evil things as the devil instigates him, even to the extent that he gives his heart, then the demon will eventually subdue him. Demons are evil spirits, but they are not spiritual beings that were made by God like angels. They were once human beings who lived on this earth. Some of the people who died without salvation come out to this world in special cases and act as the tools of the evil spirits.

The world of evil spirits was formed with Lucifer as their leader, and they disturb the works of God. Their efforts are devoted to leading just one more soul to the path to Hell. The reason why God gave Lucifer and the evil spirits the power of darkness is to gain true children through the human cultivation. True children are those who live in the Light and truth resembling God. They believe in God, the Savior Jesus Christ, and love and obey God out of volition.

The world of evil spirits can be likened to fertilizer that the farmer puts on the field. Chemical fertilizers are agents that have some toxicity and are harmful to men if ingested. But if they are supplied to the crops, they help the crops bear good yields. Similarly, through the workings of Lucifer and the evil spirits that stand against God and lead God's children to commit sins, we come to realize in a clear comparison just how filthy darkness is and how precious the Light is. Then we increasingly come to yearn for the Light more and desire to become children of the Light. Consequently, Lucifer and evil spirits are helping with human cultivation of God.

God gave men choice through freewill so that they could choose between light and darkness on their own. God dwells in the light and it is natural for those who love God to want to be in the Light and closer to God. It is through this process that God gains true children. This process is human cultivation. God is the true Light and those who turn from darkness and enter into the Light come to resemble God. These are the people who can be said to be true children of God. They will live with the Lord forever in the space of light. They will enjoy happiness and glory given by God forever.

Areas of Light and Darkness Coexist in Second Heaven

The space of light is governed by God. The space of light includes Eden in the second heaven, the third heaven that houses the kingdom of heaven, and the fourth heaven that is the original area of God.

In the second heaven, the area of light and the area of darkness coexist. As explained above, God separated light and darkness on the first day of creation. Lucifer and the evil spirits were released on the first day, and they came to dwell in the area of darkness in the second heaven from the second day of creation. God has allowed for them to stay in this area of darkness in second heaven during the course of human cultivation.

Now, what kinds of spaces are there in the area of light in second heaven?

One of them is the place for the Seven-year Wedding Banquet that the Lord has prepared. The saved souls, who are the fruit of human cultivation, will attend this Banquet in the future. 1 Thessalonians 4:17 says, *"Then we who are alive and remain will be caught up together with them in the clouds to meet the Lord in the air, and so we shall always be with the Lord."* The 'air' in this verse is this space in the area of light in the second heaven.

The other area in the area of light is the Garden of Eden. Many people think the garden was on the Earth. So, some of them searched for Israel and other parts of the Middle East. But nobody has ever found any trace of the Garden of Eden so far. It is because the Garden of Eden was not made on the Earth, but in the second heaven which is in the spiritual realm.

God made the first man, Adam, on the Earth and later led him into the Garden of Eden. This is because Adam was made of dust from the ground, but he was not a physical being. Genesis 2:7 says, *"Then the LORD God formed man of dust from the ground, and breathed into his nostrils the breath of life; and man became a living being."* Adam became a living being, a living spirit, because of the breath of life of God. The physical space was not suitable for this Adam who was a spiritual being, but it was the Garden of Eden which is a spiritual space located in the second heaven.

The Garden of Eden is a spiritual world, but it is different from the kingdom of heaven in the third heaven. It is a spiritual world but if the people there come down to this Earth, we can see and touch them. The environment of the Garden of Eden is similar to that of the Earth, but plants and animals do not ever die or perish for it is a spiritual realm. It is completely pure and clean and the natural environment is preserved as it is. The vastness of that area is beyond our imagination. Since Adam was a living spirit, in addition to the Earth, God made this Garden of

Eden in the second heaven for him.

Third Heaven and Fourth Heaven

The third heaven is the place where the kingdom of heaven is located. It houses the throne of God, and it is a space where God's children, who are saved through Jesus Christ, will live forever. The apostle Paul was led to the third heaven and saw Paradise. In addition, in Revelation 21, the apostle John explained in detail about the city of New Jerusalem. We can see that the kingdom of heaven is not like one open space, but it has many different places.

First, Paradise, which the apostle Paul saw, is the dwelling place for those believers who have the faith to barely receive salvation (Luke 23:42-43). Those who have greater faith than that of these people will go to the First Kingdom of Heaven, and those who have even greater faith will go into the Second Kingdom of Heaven.

Those who have cast away all forms of evil and become sanctified will go into the Third Kingdom of Heaven. Those who have not only cast away all evil but also accomplished the faith to please God, namely those who have gone into whole spirit, will go into the city of New Jerusalem where the throne of God is located. Among the different places of the third heaven, New Jerusalem shines most brightly. The brilliance decreases as you go further away from New Jerusalem. Paradise is the least bright.

But still, the first heaven in which we live cannot be compared with it. It is still more brilliant and more beautiful than even the Garden of Eden in the second heaven.

The fourth heaven is the space where God existed alone in the beginning. It is a space exclusively for God the Trinity. The location where the original God cohered as one light is in the fourth heaven. It is in the same dimension as that of the original universe. In the first, second, and third heavens there are different flows of time respectively. But in the fourth heaven we can say that the flow of time hardly exists, and there is no limitation bound by time. Also, God can do anything He wishes there, and it means there is no limitation of space.

Nobody can enter into this space at personal discretion except the Triune God. Only a couple of archangels and very special persons among those who are in New Jerusalem can go into this space with the permission of God. Nobody can even approach this space without the permission of God. If anybody does go into this space without the permission of God, his spirit would dissipate and scatter like smoke.

So far we have looked into the vast spiritual space. God divided the original one space into the first, second, third, and fourth heavens as a part of His plan to gain true children. Just as there are tier-like spaces of 'heaven', there are also tiered spaces that belong to the spaces of 'earth'. They are the Upper Grave, Lower Grave, Hell, and Abyss.

Upper Grave and Lower Grave

God refers to the place that belongs to God as 'heaven', and the place that belongs to the enemy devil and Satan as 'earth'. But there is an exception, and it is the Upper Grave.

Those who are saved will stay in the Upper Grave for three days before they go into a waiting place in Paradise. The Upper Grave belongs to 'earth' rather than 'heaven' in the spiritual realm. But it does not mean that it belongs to darkness. The Upper Grave is also an area of light that belongs to God, and the enemy devil and Satan cannot enter into it. It is clearly distinguished from the Lower Grave that is under the control of the power of darkness. The Upper Grave is an area of truth and light.

But the reason why it is still said to belong to 'earth' is because it is no better than even the Garden of Eden that is in the second heaven. For this reason when the Bible mentions about those who are saved going to the Upper Grave, it says they go 'down', and not 'up'.

Genesis 37:35 reads, *"Then all his sons and all his daughters arose to comfort him, but he refused to be comforted. And he said, 'Surely I will go down to Sheol in mourning for my son.' So his father wept for him."* The 'Sheol' here refers to not the Lower Grave for those who are not saved but the Upper Grave for those who are saved.

Also 1 Samuel 28:12-13 says, *"When the woman saw Samuel, she cried out with a loud voice; and the woman spoke*

31

to Saul, saying, 'Why have you deceived me? For you are Saul.' The king said to her, 'Do not be afraid; but what do you see?' And the woman said to Saul, 'I see a divine being coming up out of the earth.'" This is the scene where the woman who was a medium was surprised when she saw the dead Samuel. Samuel was in the Upper Grave, and that is why it says he came up out of the earth.

Of course, it is not actually that this medium woman called out the spirit of Samuel. Sorcerers or mediums do not have the power to communicate with God or to call out a dead spirit. They can just contact the area of darkness and call demons.

This, however, was a special occasion. God specially brought out Samuel who was in the Upper Grave to let them know the will of God. Saul had already been forsaken by God due to his disobedience, but God gave him special grace because he was still the king of Israel, and God remembered that Samuel prayed with mourning and tears for Saul to turn from his wicked ways and disobedience when he was alive.

The reason why Samuel was in the Upper Grave is because it was before Jesus took the cross. Only after Jesus died on the cross and resurrected did He take the souls in the Upper Grave to the waiting place in Paradise. Before the resurrection of Jesus, the saved souls stayed in the Upper Grave with Abraham, the father of faith, who was in charge of that place. That is why the Bible says that the saved souls go to 'Abraham's bosom'. Luke 16:22 says, *"Now the poor man died and was carried away by the angels to Abraham's bosom; and the rich man also died and was buried."*

The Bible does not clearly distinguish between the Upper Grave and the Lower Grave, and it simply says people go down to the Sheol or otherwise known as Hades. But in the parable of the rich man and poor Lazarus, Jesus talked about the different places for those who are saved and those who are not. Lazarus was saved and went to the bosom of Abraham, namely the Upper Grave, and this place is different from the Lower Grave where the rich man went. There is a great chasm between both the places and they cannot cross it to visit each other. When we explain the spiritual realm in terms of heaven and earth, we say the Upper Grave belongs to earth, but it is certainly in the area of light that belongs to God.

Hell Contains the Lakes of Fire and Burning Sulfur

The area of darkness also has a lake of fire and a lake of brimstone (burning sulfur) in addition to the Lower Grave. When those who are not saved die, they suffer in the Lower Grave and then go into the lake of fire or the lake of burning sulfur after the Great Judgment. The judgment is done without an error by the Book of Life that has the names of those who are saved and other books that write about each one's deeds.

Revelation 20:12-15 talks about how the judgment is carried out:

> *And I saw the dead, the great and the small, standing*
> *before the throne, and books were opened; and another*
> *book was opened, which is the book of life; and the dead*
> *were judged from the things which were written in the*
> *books, according to their deeds. And the sea gave up*
> *the dead which were in it, and death and Hades gave*
> *up the dead which were in them; and they were judged,*
> *every one of them according to their deeds. Then death*
> *and Hades were thrown into the lake of fire. This is the*
> *second death, the lake of fire. And if anyone's name was*
> *not found written in the book of life, he was thrown into*
> *the lake of fire.*

'The dead' refers to those who have not accepted Jesus Christ or those who have dead faith. They will stand before the throne of God to be judged, and there are books that will be opened. Other than the Book of Life that records the names of those who are saved, there are other books that write each and every deed of the dead who are not saved. Not only all people's deeds, but also all their thoughts and what they harbored in their hearts and minds from their birth to death are recorded by angels. Those who are not saved will be judged according to the magnitude of their sins recorded in the books and receive eternal punishment.

"The sea" refers to the stage of human cultivation, which is this world. Therefore, the expression, 'the sea giving up the dead', tells us that they were cultivated on this earth. Also, it means the world will give up their dead, physical bodies for the judgment. When people die without receiving salvation, their spirits will be confined in the Lower Grave while their bodies will turn into a handful of dust somewhere on this earth. But at the Final Judgment, the spirits that were in the Lower Grave will put on the bodies that are appropriate for the judgment.

Also, it says, "and death and Hades gave up the dead which were in them." It means those who were in the Lower Grave and are destined to suffer the eternal death due to their sins will stand before God to be judged. Until the Great White Throne Judgment takes place, they receive various kinds of punishments in the Lower Grave such as being torn by insects or animals or being tortured by the messengers of hell.

After the Great Judgment, they fall into either the lake of fire or the lake of burning sulfur (Revelation 21:8). The pain given in the lake of fire is incomparably more painful than the pains inflicted in the Lower Grave. They will suffer and be salted with fire where, *"THEIR WORM DOES NOT DIE, AND THE FIRE IS NOT QUENCHED"* (Mark 9:47-49). The lake of burning sulfur is the place for those who committed grave sins such as blasphemy against the Holy Spirit and disrupting the works of the Holy Spirit. It is seven times hotter than the lake of fire.

The Abyss

The deepest part of the area of darkness is the Abyss where the evil spirits would enter. After the Lord comes back in the air, the saved children of God will have the Seven-year Wedding Banquet in the air. During the same period of time, this earth will have the time of tribulation. The evil spirits that were in the air will be driven down to this earth and take the power. The world will be swept away by the World War III, and great tragedies like hell on Earth will take place. After the Seven-year Great Tribulation is over, the evil spirits will be confined in the Abyss and the Millennium Kingdom will begin on this Earth.

The children of God who finished the Seven-year Wedding Banquet in the air will come down to this Earth with the Lord and reign with Him for a thousand years (Revelation 20:4). The Earth, which had been devastated by the Seven-year Tribulation, by then will have been renewed completely to have a beautiful environment. Towards the end of the Millennium Kingdom, the evil spirits will be released once more for a moment by the providence of God, but they will again be confined in the Abyss after the Great White Throne Judgment.

Until before the Great White Throne Judgment, Lucifer and her messengers control the Lower Grave, but after the Judgment, the Lower Grave and Hell will be operated by God's power only. The evil spirits will be thrown away like trash in the Abyss that feels very dark and cold. They will be confined in a state where they cannot move at all as if they were pressed by a huge rock. The fallen angels would be thrown away with their wings taken off as a symbol of the curse and the shame.

Being thrown away may not sound as horrifying as the pains and punishments of Hell, but it is not so. Just as the pressure becomes increasingly greater as you go deeper into water, the strength of flesh will become greater as you go deeper down in Hell. The Abyss is the deepest part of Hell, and all the fleshly energy will be condensed in that place. It is much more fearful and painful punishment to go into the Abyss than to be tortured by messengers of hell in the Lower Grave or to suffer the pain of the lake of fire or the lake of burning sulfur.

Imagine you are confined in something like a big solid concrete block being unable to move at all. You are conscious, but you can neither breathe nor even blink an eye. You are a living fossil. Being fossilized, you have to receive the different kinds of pains, the force of despair, and the pressure that pushes you down as if it would burst you open.

Lucifer was loved by God greatly before she corrupted, but she will be trapped in this eternal curse as a result of standing against God. God did not punish Lucifer as soon as she corrupted. She was also merely a creature so God could have destroyed her immediately, but He didn't, and there was a reason for it.

It is because we can come forth as God's true children thanks to the existence of Lucifer, the ruler of darkness during the course of our human cultivation. We can change into children of light who resemble God by being on the alert and praying while the enemy devil is prowling around like a roaring lion trying to find someone to devour. God wants to share eternal happiness with His children of light in New Jerusalem, which is a space of light. Now, what are the qualifications to enter into this space of light?

Chapter 2

Qualifications to Enter the Space of Light

Light and darkness cannot coexist.
To go into the space of light
we have to resolve the problem of darkness.
The more we have fellowship with God who is Light
and have the heart of Jesus Christ,
the brighter space of light we can go into.

God Desires Children of Light

Practice Goodness with Heart of Spirit

Bear the Fruit of Righteousness with Faith

Bear the Fruit of Truthfulness with Deeds

The Fruits of the Light Lead Us to the Space of Light

M en have to go to either the space of light or the space of darkness after their lives on this Earth are over. Since the spirit of humans cannot be extinguished they have to go to either Heaven or Hell.

Concerning this, Hebrews 9:27 says, *"And inasmuch as it is appointed for men to die once and after this comes judgment..."* Also, John 5:29 says, *"...those who did the good deeds to a resurrection of life, those who committed the evil deeds to a resurrection of judgment."* The life on this earth is not the end. There is a life to come that is eternal, and once our physical life is over there are only the two alternatives. They are either going to Heaven or going to Hell.

The God of love wants everyone to receive salvation and enjoy happiness in the area of light. 1 Peter 2:9 says, *"But you are a chosen race, a royal priesthood, a holy nation, a people for God's own possession, so that you may proclaim the excellencies of Him who has called you out of darkness into His marvelous light."*

Let us check whether we can go into His marvelous area of

light as a royal priesthood.

God Desires Children of Light

The apostle Paul talks about God as follows: *"[God] alone possesses immortality and dwells in unapproachable light, whom no man has seen or can see. To Him be honor and eternal dominion! Amen"* (1 Timothy 6:16). It means God dwells in light, and He is eternal and perfect. 1 John 1:5 says, *"This is the message we have heard from Him and announce to you, that God is Light, and in Him there is no darkness at all."*

James 1:17 also says, *"...with [God] there is no variation or shifting shadow."* God is Light itself and He does not even have a shifting shadow. For this reason the Bible tells us in many parts that we also have to become men of light who resemble God.

1 Thessalonians 5:5 says, *"...for you are all sons of light and sons of day. We are not of night nor of darkness,"* and Ephesians 5:8-9 says, *"...for you were formerly darkness, but now you are Light in the Lord; walk as children of Light (for the fruit of the Light consists in all goodness and righteousness and truth)."* Matthew 5:14-16 also reads, *"You are the light of the world. A city set on a hill cannot be hidden; nor does anyone light a lamp and put it under a basket, but on the lampstand, and it gives light to all who are in the house. Let your light shine before men in such a way that they may see your good works, and glorify your Father who is in heaven."*

Light and darkness cannot coexist. To go into the space of light we have to resolve the problem of darkness.

Now, what is the darkness that we have to cast off to become children of light? Simply put, darkness refers to everything that belongs to sin. These are things of the flesh and works of the flesh, which were explained in detail in *Volume 1 of Spirit, Soul, and Body.*

The works of the flesh are sins committed in action, and the things of the flesh are the sins committed in the mind and thoughts. For example, wickedness, greed, evil and envy are all of unrighteousness as in Romans chapter 1. Also, as in Galatians 5, immorality, impurity, sensuality, idolatry, sorcery, enmities, strife, jealousy, outbursts of anger, disputes, dissensions, factions, envying, drunkenness, and carousing are the 'works of the flesh'.

There are also things that do not seem like they are darkness to us but are evil in the sight of God. Just as darkness cannot exist before light, the sin and evil that belong to darkness will be revealed when the light of the truth is shed on them. With the Word of God who is Light, we can realize the darkness that we have not been able to realize by ourselves.

For instance, Jesus explained that He was going to die in Jerusalem soon, and Peter tried to stop Him because of his love for Him. Then, Jesus rebuked him saying, *"Get behind Me, Satan!"* (Matthew 16:23).

Peter thought it was his duty to stop Jesus, but it was

darkness in the sight of God. It was the will of God for Jesus to be crucified and accomplish the way of salvation. With such a rebuke, Peter became a humble apostle who revived the dead and brought thousands of people to repentance in a single day after he received the Holy Spirit.

As explained, for anyone to go into the area of light, he has to come out from the world of darkness and act as a child of Light. Let us look into what we have to do more specifically.

Attain to the Righteousness of God with Faith

In order for us to go into the space of light, we first have to repent of the sin of not believing in God and then accept Jesus Christ. Whoever receives the forgiveness of sins by believing in Jesus Christ will have the qualification to enter into the space of light. Romans 3:22 says, *"...even the righteousness of God through faith in Jesus Christ for all those who believe; for there is no distinction."*

Also, John 14:6 says, *"Jesus said to him, 'I am the way, and the truth, and the life; no one comes to the Father but through Me.'"* Romans 10:9 says, *"...that if you confess with your mouth Jesus as Lord, and believe in your heart that God raised Him from the dead, you will be saved."*

If we confess with our mouth Jesus as the Lord and believe in heart that God raised Him from the dead, it means we believe in the providence of the cross and the power of resurrection. Namely, we believe that Jesus died on the cross in place of us, who as sinners were destined to receive eternal punishment due to sins, and that He shed His precious blood to redeem us from all our sins.

If we really believe in this fact, we will confess all our sins and decide to live in the light with thanks for the Lord who suffered for us. God washes away the sins of such people with the blood of the Lord and gives them the gift of the Holy Spirit. God acknowledges them as His children and writes their names in the book of life (Revelation 20:15, 21:27). This is how we can enjoy eternal life in Heaven, which is a space of light, when we acknowledge that we did not live by the Word of God, turn away from sins, and walk in the Light.

Have Fellowship with God Who Is Light

1 John 1:6-7 says, *"If we say that we have fellowship with Him and yet walk in the darkness, we lie and do not practice the truth; but if we walk in the Light as He Himself is in the Light, we have fellowship with one another, and the blood of Jesus His Son cleanses us from all sin."* Once we accept Jesus Christ and receive the gift of the Holy Spirit, we have to learn and practice the Word of God which is the truth to be considered as a child who has fellowship with God.

1 John 2:3 says, *"By this we know that we have come to know Him, if we keep His commandments,"* and 1 John 3:23 says, *"This is His commandment, that we believe in the name of His Son Jesus Christ, and love one another, just as He*

commanded us."

We have to cast away not only sins committed in action but also the evil in our hearts in obedience to God's words that tell us what we should not do and cast away. Also, we have to diligently practice the words of God that tell us to rejoice, give thanks, love, humble ourselves, serve others, and keep the commandments. It is in this way that we can cultivate the heart of the Lord with the grace and strength of God and the help of the Holy Spirit.

Our heavenly dwelling place will differ according to the exOur heavenly dwelling place will differ according to the extent to which we become sanctified, and according to how much light we emanate having become a spiritually good person through having fellowship with God who is the Light. Therefore, even though we have received salvation and obtained the qualifications to enter the space of light, we have to take hold of the heavenly kingdom by force continually until we reach the highest goal, which is the city of New Jerusalem.

There are certain measurements by which we can check the extent to which we have become children of Light. They are: spiritual love that is in 1 Corinthians 13; the nine fruits of the Holy Spirit, in Galatians 5; the Beatitudes, in Matthew 5, and the fruits of the Light in Ephesians 5. Now, let us delve into the qualifications to enter the space of light, focusing on the fruits of the Light.

Practice Goodness with the Heart of Spirit

Ephesians 5:9 says, *"...the fruit of the Light consists in all goodness and righteousness and truth."*

Goodness is to have a beautiful heart that has no evilness but has only the characters of goodness. You do good deeds to those who are in need; you do not just harm others; and you obey the Word of God and do all your best in all the work given to you, for you know about God the Creator as we would know the grace of our parents.

In the world, people say you are good if you do not react to evil with evil, but bear with it. But if you still have discomfort or hatred in your mind, can you be considered to be really good? The goodness of men and the goodness of God are very different. The first level of goodness that God recognizes is not to pay back evil with evil but to have no uncomfortable feelings at all.

It was the case with Joseph, the husband of the Virgin Mary. Matthew 1:19 says, *"And Joseph her husband, being a righteous man and not wanting to disgrace her, planned to send her away secretly."* How miserable Joseph must have felt when he found that his fiancée Mary was pregnant without having slept with him? Usually, people would have suffered so much in heart or argued with her. But Joseph had no evil in his heart, and he just wanted to leave her quietly.

The second level of goodness is, when somebody acts in evil towards us, we not only have no uncomfortable feelings, but we are able to move his heart with good words and deeds. The enemy devil and Satan cannot do anything with such a person who has reached this level of goodness.

Despite having no fault of his own, David was being chased by King Saul for a long time when one day he had a perfect opportunity to kill Saul. David had gone out to the battles and won victories for the country, but Saul would not even thank him but became jealous of him. He pursued David with his army and tried to kill him.

One day Saul went into a cave in which David was hiding. David could have killed him but he just cut off the edge of Saul's robe. Later, when Saul left the cave, he called out to Saul and said, *"Now, my father, see! Indeed, see the edge of your robe in my hand! For in that I cut off the edge of your robe and did not kill you, know and perceive that there is no evil or rebellion in my hands, and I have not sinned against you, though you are lying in wait for my life to take it"* (1 Samuel 24:11).

David called Saul, who was chasing him to kill him. He called out saying 'my father' and he truly humbled himself. He really wanted to comfort the heart of Saul saying that he was like a dog and a flea, and he did not have any intention to kill Saul. Saul was evil, but when he heard such profession coming out of goodness, he was moved and shed tears. In 1 Samuel 24:16-17 it says, *"'Is this your voice, my son David?' Then Saul lifted up his voice and wept. He said to David, 'You are more righteous than I;*

for you have dealt well with me, while I have dealt wickedly with you.'"

He was touched and just went to his home. If we pay back evil not with evil but with goodness, Satan cannot work anymore and even evil persons will be moved. Of course, Saul was so evil that his evil came out later again, but at least in that moment darkness went away by the light of David's goodness and Saul turned away.

Yet there is a higher level of goodness than just to move the heart of others. It is to love even our enemies and give our lives even for those who act evil towards us. It is the goodness of God who sent His only begotten Son, and it is the goodness of Jesus Christ. He is the holy Son of God and yet gave His life for all mankind.

We can feel this level of goodness through Moses and Paul, too. When God was about to destroy all sons of Israel due to their sins, Moses prayed that they would be saved even if it meant his name would be blotted out of the book of life (Exodus 32:32). The apostle Paul said, *"For I could wish that I myself were accursed, separated from Christ for the sake of my brethren, my kinsmen according to the flesh"* (Romans 9:3).

Stephen was martyred by being stoned while preaching the gospel. He did not have any resentment even though he was being stoned without having any fault. But rather he cried to the Lord with a loud voice, *"Lord, do not hold this sin against them!"* (Acts 7:60)

Today people think you will only suffer losses and be treated as fools if you are honest or nice to others. But God is goodness itself, and He protects us with His blazing eyes, fiery walls of the Holy Spirit, and heavenly host and angels when we follow goodness. Thus, tests and trials go away, and even if they come, we pass them with goodness. This brings to us greater blessings and prosperity in everything.

Of course, we sometimes have to sacrifice ourselves and expend our efforts to follow goodness. But those who are good do not consider such things to be difficult. They rather find it more joyful to practice goodness. Spiritual strength is to have no sin, and our spiritual light will become stronger to the extent that we cast away evil and cultivate goodness. Once we go into the level of goodness that God acknowledges, the evil one cannot even touch us because of our light, and we will be able to destroy the schemes of the enemy devil and Satan (1 John 5:18).

Bear the Fruit of Righteousness with Faith

The second of the fruit of the Light is righteousness. Generally, righteousness is to work for the right cause with one's life, without seeking one's own. But righteousness in the truth is to cast away sins, keep the commandments in the Bible, and seek God's kingdom and His righteousness in accordance with His will. Daniel is one of the best examples of having great righteousness.

Daniel was from a royal family of the tribe of Judah. He was taken captive in 605 BC when the southern kingdom of Judah was invaded by King Nebuchadnezzar of Babylon. When Babylon was recruiting talented men from other races, Daniel was chosen along with his three friends and he worked as a high official of Babylon for a long time. Although he was a captive, he had a high position in Babylon and also he was recognized as a true prophet of God. The reason is because he relied on God completely and kept his faith.

When he first went before the king of Babylon, he was a young man. He had to be trained for three years and was subject to accepting the choice food given by the king. But he was afraid that the choice food might have included the detestable foods prohibited by God, and he did not want to take it. He did not really have a choice being a captive, but he still hated and refused what God hated.

In order to keep their faith in God and not to defile themselves, he asked the overseer to allow for him along with his three friends to take only vegetables instead of king's choice food. He suggested that he take only vegetables and water for ten days as a test. When the overseer compared him with other young men after ten days, he could see that Daniel and his three friends' appearances were better than other young men.

God saw their faith and gave them amazing blessings. Daniel 1:17 says, *"As for these four youths, God gave them knowledge and intelligence in every branch of literature and wisdom; Daniel even understood all kinds of visions and dreams."* Verse 20 says, *"As for every matter of wisdom and understanding about which the king consulted them, he found them ten times better than all the magicians and conjurers who were in all his realm."*

Babylon was destroyed by Media and Persia in 539 BC during the reign of King Belshazzar, the son of King Nebuchadnezzar. A new nation, the Persian Empire, replaced Babylon. King Darius of Persia wanted to appoint Daniel as the minister to govern the whole country for Daniel possessed an extraordinary spirit. Daniel was a captive, but even when the nations and kings were changed, he was still favored the most.

Other ministers and leaders were jealous of him and tried to find a way to accuse him (Daniel 6:4-5). But they could not find any fault with him, and they suggested an ordinance to the king. Pretending that they were in support of the king, they said they would put anyone in lion's den if he prayed to any other god or man other than the king for thirty days. It was a trap they made specifically for Daniel knowing that he prayed three times a day facing Jerusalem with his windows open.

Knowing this situation, Daniel still prayed three times a day on his knees (Daniel 6:10). He could have compromised to keep his fame and power or just to avoid death, but he relied on God completely. He was eventually thrown into the lion's den for his violation of the injunction, but he did not have any resentment against his king. But he rather blessed the king saying, "O king, live forever!" He practiced righteousness no matter how difficult the situation was.

He did not have any fault or blame before God and men, and for this reason the enemy devil and Satan could not harm him with any kind of scheme. God sent His angel to protect him. He came out of the den alive and gave glory to God. The kind of righteousness that God desires of us is to keep our faith and not compromise even in the face of death and to follow goodness in truth no matter how others are acting towards us.

Bear the Fruit of Truthfulness with Deeds

The third of the fruit of the Light is truthfulness. Truthfulness is to be unchanging. It is also purity, honesty, and innocence without having any falsehood, cunningness, or craftiness. Even if you diligently do good deeds and confess your faith, it cannot be recognized as true fruit of the Light by God as long as you are doing them to flaunt yourself before others. In other words, what God wants from us is true confession of faith, true deeds, and unchanging truthfulness that comes from our heart.

In Genesis 22, we can see how Abraham obeyed the Word of God when He told him to sacrifice his only son Isaac as a burnt offering. Early in the morning he set out with Isaac to go to the land God had appointed. He had no hesitation at all. He did not have any conflict in his mind using his own thoughts. At the moment he was about to give Isaac as a burnt offering, the angel of God appeared to him and told him not to touch the lad. God said, *"...now I know that you fear God"* (Genesis 22:12).

Hebrews 11:19 says, *"He considered that God is able to raise people even from the dead, from which he also received him back as a type."* Abraham begot his son Isaac by the power

51

of God through Sarah, who was well past the age of conceiving and bearing children. So, he believed that God would revive Isaac after he gave him up as a burnt offering. We can see the firm trust between God and Abraham through this event.

On many other occasions we can see how truthful Abraham was. When he arrived at Bethel with his nephew Lot, the number of flocks and cattle was so great that their shepherds often had quarrels. Here, Abraham yielded to his nephew saying, *"Is not the whole land before you? Please separate from me; if to the left, then I will go to the right; or if to the right, then I will go to the left"* (Genesis 13:9).

Lot went to the field of Jordan that had enough water, seeking his own good, and he reached Sodom. The city of Sodom was attacked and many were taken as captives. Upon hearing this news Abraham led his men under him and brought back Lot and the people of Sodom. The king of Sodom offered him treasures, but he refused to take any of it (Genesis 14:15-23).

When Sodom and Gomorrah were destroyed by the fire from heaven, Lot and his two daughters were saved thanks to the prayers of Abraham (Genesis 18). Also, when Abraham purchased the gravesite for his wife Sarah, the Hittites offered their land and the cave of Machpelah to him, but he bought it with a fair price (Genesis 23:16). He had many children from his second wife, and while he was still alive he gave them each gifts so that they would not have any conflicts later. From all these we can see the truthfulness Abraham had.

James 2:23-24 says, *"...and the Scripture was fulfilled which says, 'And Abraham believed God, and it was reckoned to him as righteousness,' and he was called the friend of God. You see that a man is justified by works and not by faith alone."* God is truthfulness itself, and God blessed Abraham for his deeds of faith. Abraham came to dwell near the throne of God in the brightest of the space of light being the friend of God.

The Fruit of the Light Leads Us to Space of Light

For the good deeds to be seen as the fruit of the Light, it must contain righteousness, which is the righteousness of God. But having goodness and righteousness is not complete. There must be truthfulness in them. So, we can bear the fruit of the Light only when we have all of the goodness, righteousness, and truthfulness.

Now, in order for us to bear the fruit of the Light completely, we need to go through the process of coming out from darkness to enter into light, through rebukes. It is as said in Ephesians 5:11-13 KJV, *"And have no fellowship with the unfruitful works of darkness, but rather reprove them. For it is a shame even to speak of those things which are done of them in secret. But all things that are reproved are made manifest by the light: for whatsoever doth make manifest is light."*

Here, reproving is not just to rebuke the wrongdoing. It is a reproof to make one come out of darkness and into the light. Sometimes, when the church members are in difficult situations

53

due to their sins, rather than trying to comfort them I let them understand why they are facing the tests or trials. I reproved them of not living in the truth. But even though nobody is reproving us, it is important that we reprimand ourselves according to the Word of God when we have done something wrong.

When God reveals and points out each of our sins and darkness, it is because He loves us. The God of love wants His children to dwell in the perfect light of God so that they will receive blessings on this earth and furthermore they will dwell in a brighter space of light in eternal kingdom of Heaven in the future. For this, we have to cast away whatever belongs to darkness and cultivate holiness and perfection so that we can resemble God who is Light (Matthew 5:48; 1 Peter 1:16).

From the time that he met the Lord while on his way to Damascus, the apostle Paul made himself obedient to Christ and preached the gospel to innumerable Gentiles. He said, *"I affirm, brethren, by the boasting in you which I have in Christ Jesus our Lord, I die daily"* (1 Corinthians 15:31).

If we thoroughly cast away fleshly thoughts that are hostile towards God and die in the Lord daily, and have only spiritual thoughts like, "How can I accomplish the kingdom of God and His righteousness? How can I lead more souls to Heaven?" that is when we will be able to enjoy true peace and bear the fruit of the Light abundantly.

The fruit of the Light is not just about all goodness,

righteousness, and truthfulness, but it is about all kinds of the fruits that we bear by having fellowship with God and having the heart of Jesus Christ, which include spiritual love, the fruits of the Beatitudes, and the fruit of the Holy Spirit. All those fruits must be borne fully in us for us to be able to go into New Jerusalem. If some fruits are fully ripened while others are not, we will not have the qualifications to enter New Jerusalem. I hope you will all diligently practice the Word of God and have the qualifications to enter the brightest part of the space of light.

Part 2

Spirit, Soul, and Body in the Spiritual Space

Criteria in Categorization of Heavenly Dwelling Places

Glory Given in the Spiritual Space

"Behold, I tell you a mystery; we will not all sleep,
but we will all be changed, in a moment,
in the twinkling of an eye, at the last trumpet;
for the trumpet will sound,
and the dead will be raised imperishable,
and we will be changed.
For this perishable must put on the imperishable,
and this mortal must put on immortality."
- 1 Corinthians 15:51-53

Chapter 1
Different Dwelling Places

The heavenly dwelling place we will receive will differ
according to the extent to which we resemble God
and live by His will.
The heavenly kingdom has different dwelling places.
The better the heavenly dwelling place is,
the greater the honor and happiness we can enjoy there.

Heaven Has Many Dwelling Places

Heaven Suffers Violence

The Reason Why Heavenly Dwelling Places Are Categorized

Paradise, the Dwelling place for Those Who Are Barely Saved

New Jerusalem, the Dwelling place for Persons of Whole Spirit

Men have a tendency to believe something only if they can see and check it with their own eyes. But there are many things that men cannot really check with their eyes. For example, winds and the scent of flowers cannot be seen but they do exist. There is also a spiritual realm which is at a higher level of dimension than this visible, physical world. It is not right to deny the spiritual realm only because it is not visible.

In the vast spiritual space, the kingdom of heaven is located in the third heaven. The third heaven is a limitless space of light and has several different dwelling places from Paradise to New Jerusalem. The heavenly dwelling place given to each one who is saved will differ according to the extent to which each person accomplished sanctification and lived by the will of God in faith. And according to the extent that we become the kind of person that God desires in this life, we will receive a different glory as a person who belongs to Heaven.

That's why 1 Corinthians 15:40-41 reads, *"There are also heavenly bodies and earthly bodies, but the glory of the heavenly is one, and the glory of the earthly is another. There is one glory of the sun, and another glory of the moon, and another glory of the stars; for star differs from star in glory.*"

The Individual Glories in Heaven

One of God's original natures is holiness. The Bible often talks about holiness because God wants men who are created in God's image to have the holiness of God. Leviticus 20:26 says, *"Thus you are to be holy to Me, for I the LORD am holy; and I have set you apart from the peoples to be Mine."* 1 Peter 1:16 says, *"...because it is written, 'You shall be holy, for I am holy.'"*

Therefore, those who live by the will of the holy God are the ones who belong to heaven. They will enjoy the heavenly glory in the heavenly kingdom. On the other hand, those who live in sins and evil, which is against the will of God, are the ones who belong to the earth, and consequently, they will go to Hell.

The ones who belong to the earth are not just the people who do not accept Jesus Christ and do not believe in God. In Matthew 7:21 it says, *"Not everyone who says to Me, 'Lord, Lord,' will enter the kingdom of heaven, but he who does the will of My Father who is in heaven will enter."* Even if they say, 'Lord, Lord,' and say that they believe in Him, they are still among those who belong to the earth as long as they do not practice the will of God.

What do we have to do to go into the heavenly kingdom and enjoy the glory of the sun as a person who belongs to heaven? In Hebrews 12:4 we find that during our life on this earth, we have to struggle against and cast away all our sins 'to the point of shedding blood'. Furthermore, in 1 Thessalonians 5:22 it says that we have to accomplish holiness by getting rid of all forms of evil and being full of the Spirit. Just as the light of the sun, the light of the moon, and the light that the stars give out are all different, the glory of the persons who belong to heaven will be different as well.

Isaiah 60:1 says, *"Arise, shine; for your light has come, and the glory of the LORD has risen upon you."* After we accept Jesus Christ who came as the Light of the world, we come to emanate spiritual lights to the extent that we act by the Word of God. As persons who belong to heaven, we ought to give out the light as bright as the sunshine at noon so that we can drive away the power of darkness, lead the souls to the way of salvation, and give glory to God.

Heaven Has Many Dwelling Places

Jesus had the Passover supper with His disciples in the upper room at Mark's right before His death. At the Last Supper, He reminded them of the existence of the kingdom of heaven so that they would have hope for it.

Jesus said in John 14:2-3, *"In My Father's house are many dwelling places; if it were not so, I would have told you; for I go to prepare a place for you. If I go and prepare a place for you, I will come again and receive you to Myself, that where I am, there you may be also."*

61

Jesus resurrected on the third day after He was crucified and ascended into Heaven in the view of many people. He went to prepare the dwelling places in Heaven where God's children will dwell forever. When He said, *"In My Father's house are many dwelling places,"* He expresses the desire that all men should be saved (1 Timothy 2:4).

Heaven is a spiritual space that was created even before God the Trinity created the Earth. It is a limitless space whose depth, width, density, and volume cannot be measured with the human mind. It has the throne of God, countless spiritual beings, and the homes where the children of God will live forever. At the center of the kingdom of heaven is New Jerusalem, which is Heaven's most glorious dwelling place.

The spiritual lights that flow from the throne of God and the river of water of life make the children of God feel happier and more honored. God gives each of us an appropriate dwelling place and rewards us according to what kind of faith we had and how we gave glory to God on this earth.

The city of New Jerusalem is located at the apex of the third heaven, and 'below' New Jerusalem are the Third, Second, and First Kingdoms of Heaven, and Paradise. It does not mean, however, that they are layered like a building on this earth with one literally above another. All dwelling places in Heaven are horizontal and yet vertical having different heights.

Heaven Suffers Violence

Matthew 11:12 says, *"From the days of John the Baptist until now the kingdom of heaven suffers violence, and violent men take it by force."* Heaven is a beautiful and peaceful place, and why does it say it suffers violence, and violent men take it by force?

It means those who have greater hope for the heavenly kingdom will lead a diligent life in faith and try to enter into the city of New Jerusalem. This diligent life is referred to by the expression 'violent men take it by force'.

Now, who do they have to be violent against? They are violent against the enemy devil and Satan that instigate men to commit sins. In order to go into Heaven, we have to fight the darkness and overcome it. To cause men to fall, the enemy Satan stimulates the sinful natures in men and causes them to commit sins. Here, those who really long for the kingdom of heaven will overcome it with the Word of God.

We can take the city of New Jerusalem by force to the extent that we become holy children of God by means of the Word of God and prayer (1 Timothy 4:5). From 2 Corinthians 12:1 onward, we see the apostle Paul went to Paradise, which is in the third heaven, and learned great secrets of the kingdom of heaven. From that time on he kept on fighting the good fight until he became a martyr. He took the city of New Jerusalem by force, looking up to the crown of righteousness that God prepared for him.

Revelation 19:7-8 reads, *"Let us rejoice and be glad and give the glory to Him, for the marriage of the Lamb has come and His bride has made herself ready. It was given to her to clothe herself in fine linen, bright and clean; for the fine linen is the righteous acts of the saints,"* and Revelation 22:14 also reads, *"Blessed are those who wash their robes, so that they may have the right to the tree of life, and may enter by the gates into the city."*

Here, the 'robes' and 'fine linen' refer to the heart and deeds of men. We can pass through the gates and go into the holy city only when we purify our hearts and deeds. As the plural 'gates' are used, we can see that there are many gates. In order for us to enter New Jerusalem, we first have to go through the gate of salvation and acquire the qualifications to enter Paradise. Then, we have to pass through the gates of the First, Second, and Third Kingdoms of Heaven. Lastly, we have to pass through the Pearl Gates of New Jerusalem.

This is the reason why it says 'gates', and we can learn from this passage that not all who are saved will receive the same glory in Heaven. It is something for which we should be very thankful that we know about this heavenly kingdom and strive to take better dwelling places by force.

The Reason Why Heavenly Dwelling Places Are Categorized

Those who have accepted Jesus Christ, but do not circumcise their heart and thus have not cast away evil, have a spiritual light that is very dim. But those who have cast away all forms of evil and have become sanctified have very strong spiritual light. As stated earlier, each believer has a different brightness of his spiritual light. The more believers practice the Word of God and cast away sins, the brighter and the more beautiful is the light that emanates from them. Those who have become completely sanctified have such bright lights that those who have not cannot even look directly at them.

If we just think with common sense of men, we can easily understand that it is difficult for those who have strong spiritual light and those who do not to mingle and live together. Even on this earth, it is more comfortable for children to gather with children, teenagers with teenagers, and grown adults with grown adults. Children and grown adults cannot really become friends because the worlds they live in are different, and their intelligence and ways of thinking are all significantly different.

Similarly, those who have similar brightness of spiritual light will dwell in the same place. What if everybody lived in one same space in the eternal kingdom of heaven? Those who are sanctified will understand each other's hearts and they would have no inconveniences. But those who are not sanctified cannot really understand them. For this reason, God categorized several different dwelling places so that people with similar magnitudes of spiritual brightness can dwell comfortably together.

Revelation 21:23 says, *"And the city has no need of the sun or of the moon to shine on it, for the glory of God has illumined it, and its lamp is the Lamb."* Among the several heavenly dwelling places, the city of New Jerusalem is the crystalloid of human cultivation that God planned. It is the place where God can share love with His children forever. God has prepared the Third, Second, and First Kingdoms of Heaven, and Paradise for those who do not completely cultivate hearts of truth and are not qualified to enter New Jerusalem.

Now, let us delve into some of the characteristics of each dwelling place from Paradise to the city of New Jerusalem. We'll also look at what kinds of people go into each dwelling place.

Paradise, the Dwelling Place for Those Who Are Barely Saved

God sent Jesus to this earth for us who were going the way of death due to sins. Jesus redeemed us from all our sins through His crucifixion. If we believe that He is the only way to salvation and accept Him as our personal Savior, God gives us the gift of the Holy Spirit. Once we receive the Holy Spirit, our spirit that had been dead due to Adam's sin will be revived, and we receive the right to call God our 'Father'. It means we become children of God, our names are written in the Book of Life, and we are given citizenship in the heavenly kingdom.

But after our dead spirit has been revived, this spirit cannot grow if we do not practice the Word of God and cast away sins. Our spirit grows to the extent that we cast off sins. We can go into New Jerusalem only when we have fully recovered the lost image of God by making our spirit grow completely. If our spirit does not grow up and if we barely receive salvation having faith as small as a mustard seed, then we will go to Paradise. In terms of the levels of faith, this is faith at the very first level. The first level of faith is the level with which we receive salvation with shame.

Paradise is a place that is made with love and compassion of God. God has prepared this place for people who are saved but are not worthy to be called God's children. It is somewhat shameful to call them God's children but God cannot send them to Hell either. But in fact, Paradise will accommodate the most number of believers of all the other dwelling places. This place is even wider than the universe of the first heaven. The people of Paradise will be thankful and live happily forever just for the fact that they did not go to Hell but were saved.

Even though it is the lowest level dwelling place of Heaven, there is still no place on earth that has the beauty and magnificence to begin to compare with it. On the wide plain that has perfect harmony of beautiful flowers and green trees, various animals wander about and all of these animals look lovely.

On this earth, the trees and flowers will wither and perish

with the passage of time. But, the trees of Paradise are always green and the flowers there never wither. As people approach them, the flowers will sway back and forth or open and close their buds as they give out unique and wonderful fragrances as if they were welcoming the people. There are so many kinds of fruits. They are a little bigger than those of this earth and have an aurora of brilliance. People can eat them right from the tree because there is no dust or insects.

They can sit on the grass lawn and have friendly conversations while eating the fruit. These people have not done anything for the kingdom of God during their earthly lives, so they do not receive any reward in Heaven. But they are so happy just for the fact that there is no sorrow, disease, pain, or death. In very exceptional cases and occasions, some of them can be invited to events held in New Jerusalem.

But there is a great difference of light between those who are in New Jerusalem and those who are in Paradise, so the people in Paradise do not usually accept the invitation for they are too embarrassed to go. When they do visit, they have to follow specific orders and timing. They will be so happy just by visiting the glorious city of New Jerusalem, and it is a great joy to share what they have seen and experienced in New Jerusalem after returning to Paradise.

Just because Paradise is the lowest level dwelling place in Heaven, we must not underestimate the beauty and happiness of it. Though it is a place for those who are saved with shame, it is still a place that cannot be compared with any place on this earth in beauty, and it is even more beautiful than the Garden of Eden where Adam lived.

First Kingdom of Heaven

The First Kingdom of Heaven is a more beautiful and happier place than Paradise. Everything is environmentally more beautiful than Paradise. This is a place for those who have accepted Jesus Christ, made their dead spirits revived, and have tried to put the Word of God into action but have not practiced it completely. Namely, it is for those who have the second level of faith in the growth process of faith.

In the First Kingdom of Heaven, they receive rewards and a house according to what they have done on this earth. The houses in the First Kingdom of Heaven are like apartments on this earth. But they are built with gold and other precious gem stones according to the tastes of the owners. There are elevators in the buildings, which are run by the power of God, and they take you to the floor you want without having to press a button.

For those who go into the First Kingdom of Heaven, an imperishable crown will be given (1 Corinthians 9:25). It is like a participation prize. They knew the Word of God but did not practice it on this earth. They knew they had to cast off sins but they did not cast off many of their sins of commission. But God considers their effort itself to practice His Word as their faith and gives them rewards accordingly.

There are many beautiful gardens in the First Kingdom of Heaven. There are also recreational facilities such as big parks with a lot of trees, amusement parks, lakes, trails for walking, swimming pools, golf courses, tennis courts, etc. But except the individual places to live and the crowns that are given, everything else is for public use. It's similar to having parks or sports facilities in apartment complexes for public use.

There are no personally-ministering angels. However, the people can receive the guidance of angels everywhere. This is what primarily differentiates it from Paradise. For example, while they are talking on a bench, they can ask an angel to get some fruits for them if they want fruit to eat. But in Paradise, they have to get the fruits by themselves. This way, there is a great difference in the way of living between those who are in Paradise and those in the First Kingdom of Heaven. Those who are in the First Kingdom of Heaven do not become jealous of those who are living in higher level dwelling places. Everyone feels the utmost happiness and satisfaction at each dwelling place.

Second Kingdom of Heaven

The Second Kingdom of Heaven is even brighter and more beautiful than the First Kingdom of Heaven. The buildings that are built with precious stones are more splendid and beautiful. The number of different kinds of animals and plants are more diverse than in Paradise and the First Kingdom of Heaven. Even the same kind of animal or plant is much more beautiful than those of the First Kingdom of Heaven. In the case of animals, the physical grace is more elegant and the beauty is more splendid, and the colors of the feathers and fur are more brilliant. It's the same with the aroma and colors of flowers.

The Second Kingdom of Heaven is for those who practiced the Word of God in action, but have not fully accomplished sanctification, namely for those who are in the third level of faith. They cast away all sins in action but did not completely cast off all sins committed in thoughts and sins of the heart.

They will be given a single-story individual house, and they will have a nameplate on the gate. These houses are so much more beautiful and grand than any mansion of this earth. The commonly given reward other than the house is the crown of glory. They gave glory to God on this earth to some extent, and that is why God gives them the crown of glory (1 Peter 5:4).

In addition to the crown and the house, those who go into the Second Kingdom of Heaven can have something individually that they most desire. If they want to have a swimming pool, they can have a wonderful swimming pool made with beautiful gemstones. If they want a lake, they can have it. If they want a ballroom, they can have one. If they like taking a walk, they can have trails for walking that have many plants and flowers along the path and many lovely animals wander around.

Since everybody has different tastes, there are all kinds of different facilities, so they can visit each other's homes to see and use those different facilities together. In Heaven everybody serves everybody, and so no one refuses anybody who might

71

come to his/her house to visit. But rather, they become happier for they can share what they have. The visitors do not seek their own advantages either, so they make visits within the boundaries of being polite.

Those who are in the Second Kingdom of Heaven do not feel sorry for or envy what other people have just because they have only one facility. But they are rather thankful that God has given them such a great reward which is much more than what they did on this earth. One thing that is in their mind is that they did not completely sanctify themselves during their lives on this earth. They will be so embarrassed for the fact that they did not cast off evil completely that they too cannot lift up their faces before God.

Third Kingdom of Heaven

The difference of glory between the Second Kingdom of Heaven and the Third Kingdom of Heaven is like difference between the heavens and the earth. This difference stems from whether or not an individual accomplished sanctification. Those who are in the Third Kingdom of Heaven are at the fourth level of faith. They accomplished holiness so they can have all kinds of facilities they want as their reward. They can have golf courses, swimming pools, and ballrooms—that is, they can have anything they want so they don't have to use the facility at somebody else's house.

The houses have multiple stories, and they are so grand and

fancy that even billionaires on this earth cannot imitate such houses. They have vast gardens filled with fragrant flowers and trees that are beautifully decorated. Fish of many kinds and colors swim in the lakes that radiate brilliantly dazzling lights. Of course, these houses are less than those in New Jerusalem in terms of the size, beauty, and glory. Speaking in terms of ratio, if we say the land of the smallest house in New Jerusalem is 100 units, that of the largest home in the Third Kingdom of Heaven is only 60 units. This tells us that God is so delighted with those who enter into New Jerusalem.

The houses in the Third Kingdom of Heaven give out beautiful aroma and lights to the extent that the house owner resembles God. The common factor of houses in both the Third Kingdom of Heaven and New Jerusalem is that they do not have nameplates. The houses themselves give out unique fragrance and an aurora-like light that represents the owner, so everybody knows whose house it is without the nameplate. It is also because among all the believers who go into the heavenly kingdom, there are comparatively only a few who go into the Third Kingdom of Heaven or New Jerusalem.

It's not just about the houses. Even the same golden roads are much brighter and more precious than those of the Second Kingdom of Heaven. Because they can have all the facilities they want, in the Third Kingdom of Heaven, there are many angels given, too. There are many helping angels that manage the house and visitors. Up to the Second Kingdom of Heaven there are no personally ministering angels but in the Third Kingdom of

Heaven and New Jerusalem angels are assigned to all residents there. They also have cloud-like automobiles for public use, and they can travel the endless heavenly kingdom as they wish.

A crown of life is given to residents in the Third Kingdom of Heaven. It is a basic reward given because they passed the tests of giving their lives for the Lord (James 1:12). Those in the Third Kingdom of Heaven lived such glorious lives compared to that of those in the Second Kingdom of Heaven. But even these people have some regrets when they see New Jerusalem. Therefore, it is very important that we please God by being faithful in all God's house along with cultivating holiness in us.

New Jerusalem, the Dwelling Place for Persons of Whole Spirit

John the apostle said about the glory of the city of New Jerusalem in Revelation 21:11, *"... Her brilliance was like a very costly stone, as a stone of crystal-clear jasper."*

The whole city is surrounded by the glory of God. The lights that are emanated from the city of New Jerusalem are so dignified and beautiful that we will not be able to hold our exclamations if we see them. It is such a beautiful and magnificent place, way beyond our imagination. It is given to those who accomplished holiness completely; who were faithful in all God's house; and who followed His will with an understanding of the deep heart of God. Namely, it is a dwelling place for those persons of whole spirit who have reached the fifth level of faith.

This city is surrounded by high walls that give out brilliant lights, and this is the borderline between the Third Kingdom of Heaven and the city of New Jerusalem. The measurements of the city of New Jerusalem are the same in width, height, and length. Each of them is 12,000 stadia (Revelation 21:16). A stadium is a measure of distance, and 12,000 stadia are about 2,400km.

If you see the city of New Jerusalem horizontally, that is the length and width, the area of the city is 58 times the area of South Korea. But this calculation of the area is only two-dimensional. New Jerusalem is also 2,400km high. Therefore, we cannot fully understand the space in the city of New Jerusalem just with our concept of area.

Each of the four sides of the city wall has three pearl gates, which in total are twelve gates. The foundation stones of the city wall are twelve different kinds of precious gemstones. Each gate is guarded by an angel, and the roads are made with pure gold which is like crystal-clear glass. There are also many other precious gemstones in addition to the twelve foundation stones. Some of them are so big that we cannot imagine their size. Some others give out double or triple layers of different lights.

The interior of the city of New Jerusalem can be divided into the area of the Father God, the area of the Lord, and area of the Holy Spirit. In the area of the Father are located the houses of patriarchs of faith who were active in the Old Testament times including, but not limited to Elijah, Enoch, Moses, and Abraham. To the right and downward from the throne of God is the area of the Lord, where the main castle of the Lord that has golden roof is located. Around the castle are many other buildings of various colors and shapes. At the closest proximity are located the houses of His disciples Peter, John, and James, and then the houses of other disciples.

To the left and downward from the throne of God is the area of the Holy Spirit, which in general gives out the soft and mild feeling like that of a mother. In this area are located the houses of those who have come forth as persons of whole spirit during the era of the Holy Spirit. Some of the houses are already completed while some other houses are being decorated with beautiful jewels, and are almost complete. For some houses, their land is being enlarged, because the owner of the house is still saving more souls on this earth.

The houses in New Jerusalem are as big and splendid as giant castles. They will be given the land to the extent that they have accomplished meekness on this earth, and those who are in New Jerusalem will be given a large piece of land for their houses for they have cultivated a great deal of meekness. Each house has all the facilities that the owner wants, and one can easily tell whose house it is because it is built according to the faith, rewards, and tastes of the owner. The light of God's glory and the jewels that decorate each house tell us to what extent the owner cultivated holiness and how he/she pleased God on this earth. They are given beautiful rewards to the extent that they had given up what they liked, what they wanted to do, and what they wanted to have for the Lord.

The crown of gold and the crown of righteousness will basically be given to those who go into New Jerusalem. The crown of gold has many kinds of decorations of precious stones. Revelation 4:4 says, *"Around the throne were twenty-four thrones; and upon the thrones I saw twenty-four elders sitting, clothed in white garments, and golden crowns on their heads."*

The gold of the golden crown is pure gold that has no other foreign substance in it. It represents true faith that never changes. It is a reward given for the fact that they reached the measure of faith that pleases God.

The crown of righteousness is given to those who have cultivated pure heart that is blameless and spotless and who have been faithful to the kingdom of God (2 Timothy 4:7-8). Other than the crowns of gold and righteousness, other kinds of crowns will be given to those who go into New Jerusalem as well. For each occasion in which they greatly gave glory to God on this earth, a crown will be rewarded.

Other than these, there are many more things that God has prepared for us in the city of New Jerusalem. About this, Revelation 21:2 says, *"And I saw the holy city, new Jerusalem, coming down out of heaven from God, made ready as a bride adorned for her husband."* Just as the brides adorn themselves most beautifully on the wedding day, God has prepared the city of New Jerusalem as the most beautiful, comfortable, and coziest and happiest place among all heavenly dwelling places.

Various colors that are emanated from brilliant gemstones of each house will make a perfect harmony of colors. Some houses have a great lake, a big forest, a vast plain, a wonderfully decorated gardens, recreational facilities, countless birds and beautiful animals. Just going into New Jerusalem itself will move the heart of the people. They will enjoy happiness forever in glory and emotion that cannot be adequately described.

There are not many who have gone into New Jerusalem since the beginning of human cultivation. God wants everyone to come forth as His true children and go into New Jerusalem, but there are so many more people who are just barely saved. They are always thankful just for the fact that they did not fall into Hell, and instead, they can enjoy true rest in Paradise.

The happiness felt in Paradise cannot even begin to compare with that felt in New Jerusalem. It is also very different from the happiness felt in the First Kingdom of Heaven. There are many differences in the environments and other conditions of each heavenly dwelling place according to the justice of God, and this is actually God's loving consideration for us. He allowed for those who are at similar levels of spirit to live together so they will feel the utmost freedom and happiness in each dwelling place. In this way, people live in their respective heavenly dwelling places, and for this kind of life they have the spiritual body that is most suitable for the spiritual space.

Chapter 2

Spirit, Soul, and Body in the Spiritual Space

God's gift will be given in different measure according to
the extent to which we have cultivated spirit, soul, and body
belonging to spirit while living in this physical space.
He gives us the glory that we enjoy in our heavenly dwelling place as well as
clothes, crowns, and other decorations according to what we have done.

1. Spiritual Form

2. Soul and Body Belonging to Spirit

3. God's Gift

In movies or TV dramas we sometimes see that the spirit, that looks exactly the same as the person, comes out of the body. The spirit that has come out of the body sees the body lying down and wonders with a surprise, "Why is a person like me lying down there?" Is this kind of thing just a fiction that exists only in movies or TV dramas? The Bible writes about the existence of the spiritual realm and our spirit.

In order for us to live in the eternal kingdom of heaven later, we will have to have spirit, soul, and body that belong to spiritual space. All men are born with a spirit that is dead because of Adam's sin. As a result, they live following their lusts. But once they accept Jesus Christ and receive the Holy Spirit, their dead spirit can be revived, and they can become true children of God who long for the spiritual realm.

God created human beings and has been cultivating mankind just as a farmer sows the seeds in the field and cultivates them. Only when we understand His providence can we revive our dead spirit and make our spirit, soul, and body belong to spirit. We can enjoy life in the eternal kingdom of heaven having a complete heavenly body only when we have the spirit, soul, and body that are suitable for a life in the third heaven, which is the space of light.

What are we going to look like in this space of light? On this earth, we have the spirit, soul, and body that are suitable for the physical space. But once we go into spiritual space, we will have to have a spirit, soul, and body that are appropriate for that space.

1. Spiritual Form

Spiritual form is the shape of spirit. It can also be considered a vessel to contain the spirit. Each person who is saved has a form that belongs to heaven, and the glory of each one is different. The light of the spiritual body is different according to the measure of each one's holiness. We will have the resurrected body, and then the perfected heavenly body after that.

Form is the shape of substance. When we see an eagle flying in the sky, we can say it is an eagle because it has its unique shape. Lions have the form of a lion and eagles have the form of an eagle so we can distinguish them from each other.

The physical body is the physical form that we can perceive with our eyes. In case of men, we have a form that belongs to this earth, which is our physical body, but we can also have a spiritual form which belongs to heaven.

1 Corinthians 15:38-40 says, *"But God gives it a body just as He wished, and to each of the seeds a body of its own. All flesh is not the same flesh, but there is one flesh of men, and another flesh of beasts, and another flesh of birds, and another of fish. There are also heavenly bodies and earthly bodies, but the glory of the heavenly is one, and the glory of the earthly is another."* Just as we have a visible form which is our physical body, a spirit also has a form. We can say that spiritual form is the vessel to hold the spirit itself. As for men, when our lives on this earth are over, the contents of the soul are not extinguished but are contained in the spiritual body. The lights of the spiritual

body are different according to the extent to which one has practiced the truth on this earth. The spiritual body of each person is different, which means one body is distinguishable from another. Seeing the light of the spiritual body, we can even tell which heavenly dwelling place each person will inherit if God calls him/her right now.

The spiritual form is not a shadowy figure. Its shape is distinctly solid. Though it seems like it has weight, there is none. And yet while it feels like it has no weight, there is weight. It is like picking up a piece of fine tissue paper. It doesn't feel like there is any weight, but actually there is weight. But it does not mean that the spirit is so weak that it is something swayed by wind. It is so light that it cannot be weighed, but it is stable.

Spiritual Form of Adam

Adam is the first man that God created. God delicately made all his entrails, bones, and the whole shape of man, and he became a living being, namely a living spirit, when God breathed into his nostrils the breath of life. Adam's heart began to beat, his blood to circulate, and his organs and cells to function. He was a beautiful being that had the flesh and bones that never aged and that would never perish. Furthermore, when God breathed into him the breath of life, Adam's spirit came to have the exact same form as his physical body. Just as Adam's body had a form, his spirit also came to have a form that looked the same as his physical body. Adam's spirit that could communicate with God and his soul that could assist the spirit were contained in Adam's body.

Adam could keep the Word of God and communicate with God because his soul and body obeyed his spirit. When he was created, his spirit that was contained in the spiritual body was like a blank sheet of paper. So, God led him to the Garden of Eden and taught him the knowledge of spirit. And God said to Adam, *"...but from the tree of the knowledge of good and evil you shall not eat, for in the day that you eat from it you will surely die"* (Genesis 2:17).

After spending a long period of time in the Garden of Eden, Adam ate the forbidden fruit that Eve gave to him, which she had eaten after having been tempted by Satan. As a result, just as God had spoken the words, "You will surely die," Adam's spirit died. Thereby his communication with God was severed.

Of course, Adam's spirit came from God, so it can never be completely extinguished. The breath of life that God breathed into Adam's nostrils has the trait of imperishability. That is, it has the character of being 'never perishing.'

Here, saying that his spirit died means that the communication with God was severed and its activity came to a complete halt. As his spirit was no longer active, the soul took over the place of the master of man and it ruled over the body. Since the fall of Adam, the knowledge of spirit that kept Adam a living spirit began to leak out. Then, the fleshly attributes that belong to darkness began to come into the spiritual form. From this moment on, Adam's body was under the control of physical order. He became a being that had to change, age, and eventually face death.

The Spiritual Form of a Person at the Time of Death

As for men, after their physical bodies die, their spirit and soul will be contained in the spiritual form and they will exist forever. The soul does not get extinguished even after physical death because it is combined with the spirit and keeps on having operations of soul. Even after the body is dead and the brain functions stop, the knowledge contained in the brain will remain in the spiritual form. The thoughts and the feelings also remain. This combined spirit and soul are known as the 'spirit-soul,' but in most cases we simply refer to them as 'spirit'.

On the one hand, if one accepts Jesus Christ, lives by the Word of God, and has gained the right to go into the space of light, his spiritual form will be shining. On the other hand, if one's spirit is dead for he does not have fellowship with God who is Light but lives in sins and evil being stained by the world, his spiritual form will only have darkness.

The appearances of those who are saved and those who are not will be completely the opposite at their moment of death. Those who are not saved usually die in fear with their eyes opened, but those who are saved die in peace with their eyes closed. They come to know that there is a Heaven and there is a Hell at the moment their spirit comes out of their body.

Some of those who are not saved see that the messengers of hell are waiting for them. The messengers of hell are filled with darkness from head to toe. They are in black robes. They have pale faces, blackish-red lips, and very dark energy below their eyes. How completely full of fear one would become as messengers of hell with such grotesque appearances approach! At that moment, he comes to know that there is surely Heaven and Hell and he dies in fear. But it is too late for him. Regretting his past will not help him. He cannot escape being dragged into Hell.

But those who keep their faith and lead a good life as a Christian do not have to be afraid of anything. They see two angels in white robes who wait for them just before their deaths, so their faces are rosy and they are at peace. At the moment their spirit is separated from their body, they feel overwhelming and indescribable joy and happiness.

There was a believer who passed away after leading a life in faith in our church for some time. She was really good-hearted and so gentle that she never had any trouble or conflict with anybody. She had peace with everybody and she spoke only words of goodness, love, and truth with gentleness. She loved God fervently and so her first priority was always God's work. She did not spare her life when it was for the kingdom of God. I could see such bright lights coming out from her funeral place. When I saw the dignity of the angels who came to take her spirit, I could imagine the kind of heavenly dwelling place she would enter.

The Spiritual Form of the Saved

When a person who is saved dies on this earth, his spirit comes out of his body. Now, there are two angels who escort his spirit and guide him to the waiting place of Heaven. Before the resurrection of the Lord, the Upper Grave was the waiting place of Heaven. But after His resurrection, it has been changed. The souls (spirit-soul) stay at another waiting place on the outskirts of Paradise. Those souls who were saved during the Old Testament times were moved to this waiting place, too.

In the New Testament times, for those who are saved, when their spirits leave their body they first go to the Upper Grave. They stay there for three days to adapt themselves to the spiritual realm and receive the training and knowledge necessary for the spiritual realm. After that they are moved to the waiting place on the outskirts of Paradise. The process of human cultivation will come to an end at the second coming of the Lord in the air. After that is the Millennium Kingdom, and when this also is over, there will be the Great White Throne Judgment. Through the Judgment, God will give each person a heavenly dwelling place and the rewards according to his/her deeds.

Now, for those who are saved, what kind of appearances do their spiritual forms have? If we know about spiritual form, we can more easily understand about resurrection and the Rapture. If one dies in his childhood, his spiritual form also has the appearance of a child. If he died at his youth, his spiritual form would also appear young. If one dies as an old man, his spiritual form will also look old. But spiritual forms do not have any beards, disabilities, scars, or wrinkles. Even if one dies of a disease, his spiritual form would still be healthy and beautiful. The spiritual forms of elderly people would look similar to the appearance of the physical body at the time of death. However, they do not look frail but they have the appearance of a healthy and energetic body.

They all wear white robes and the spiritual forms themselves emanate lights. The strength of the lights is different from person to person. The more holiness one has achieved, the brighter and the more beautiful the light is. According to the brightness of the light, the heavenly dwelling place and glories given to each one will also be different. For women, the length of their hair will be different according to the measure of holiness they cultivated. 1 Corinthians 11:15 says, *"...but if a woman has long hair, it is a glory to her? For her hair is given to her for a covering."*

For those women who will go into Paradise, the First Kingdom of Heaven, or the Second Kingdom of Heaven, their hair will come down to their shoulder level. For those who go into the Third Kingdom of Heaven, it comes down to the middle part of the back, and for those who go into New Jerusalem it comes down to the waist. But for men, the length of the hair is the same, which comes down to the nape of the neck. The hair in Heaven is wavy blonde for both men and women.

The spiritual form in the waiting place of Heaven is not yet complete and perfect. They still wait for the second coming of

89

the Lord in the air, which is their time for resurrection. They can have the resurrected body only when the Lord appears in the air again.

The Resurrected Body

When the Lord comes back in the air, those souls who are in the waiting place of Heaven will be combined with their physical body that will have been resurrected from their graves. That is why the Bible says that those who died believing are not dead but asleep. Their bodies that are dead and buried will be resurrected and caught up to the air, and unite with their respective spirit-soul. We call this united body the 'resurrected body'.

If the body had turned into a handful of dust in the grave after a long period of time, or if it has been cremated, how can it be resurrected and combined with the spirit? Though invisible to our eyes, the elements that comprised the body still exist on this earth. At the coming of the Lord, all those elements will gather together and be resurrected by the power of God. This body will rendezvous with the spirit-soul and become the whole body of spirit, soul, and body.

Next, those who receive the Lord alive will also change into a spiritual body and be caught up into the air. This is called the 'Rapture'. It can be compared to a gigantic magnet pulling iron dust up into the air.

1 Thessalonians 4:16-17 says, *"For the Lord Himself will descend from heaven with a shout, with the voice of the*

archangel and with the trumpet of God, and the dead in Christ will rise first. Then we who are alive and remain will be caught up together with them in the clouds to meet the Lord in the air, and so we shall always be with the Lord."

1 Corinthians 15:51-53 says, *"Behold, I tell you a mystery; we will not all sleep, but we will all be changed, in a moment, in the twinkling of an eye, at the last trumpet; for the trumpet will sound, and the dead will be raised imperishable, and we will be changed. For this perishable must put on the imperishable, and this mortal must put on immortality."*

These saved souls will meet the Lord in the air and have a wedding banquet for seven years. Here, 'the air' refers to a special space provided at one side of Eden in the second heaven. Eden is a vast space that includes the Garden of Eden. The Seven-year Wedding Banquet is a time for saved souls to be comforted and to enjoy themselves. It is to celebrate the efforts expended during the period of human cultivation on this earth. It is also a time to give thanks to God remembering their lives on this earth.

When they change into the resurrected body, they will be able to see the degree of sanctification they had achieved in the cultivation of the heart of the Lord. They will also then have a vague understanding of the kinds of rewards and glory they will later receive at the Final Judgment. They will have the Seven-year Wedding Banquet in the air in the resurrected body, and afterwards they will come down to this earth to spend a thousand years.

So then, how is the resurrected body different from the

spiritual form? The resurrected body and the spiritual form each sense the spiritual space in a very different way. The spiritual form alone cannot be a complete body in the spiritual space. We can say one has the basic form to live in the spiritual space when he has the resurrected body. The spiritual form has the appearance of the person at the time of his death, but the resurrected body will be like that of a thirty-three year old for everybody..

Jesus finished His earthly life at the age of thirty three. Thirty-three years of age is the peak of one's life just as the sun is the brightest at noon. They would be mature enough and yet not too old to have full energy and vigor. They will have acquired a matured beauty after passing through their 20's. Compared to flowers, it is similar to the time of the full bloom.

For this reason God gave His children a spiritual body with the appearance of the age of thirty-three. The height of men will be around 190cm (about 6' 3") and for women it will be 170cm (5' 7") or so. Nobody will be too fat or too thin; everyone will have the most beautiful appearances.

The resurrected body is tangible. It can be physically felt with the hands since it is the spirit and soul combined with the resurrected physical body. Jesus Christ is the one who showed to us this resurrected body. The resurrected Lord appeared to His disciples and said, *"See My hands and My feet, that it is I Myself; touch Me and see, for a spirit does not have flesh and bones as you see that I have"* (Luke 24:39). As He said, the resurrected body has flesh and bones.

The resurrected body is also an imperishable body which is not bound by the physical limitations of this world. The resurrected Lord appeared to the disciples passing through the walls as recorded in John 20:19, 26. In John 20:22, it says Jesus 'breathed on them'. The resurrected body can breathe and also eat and drink. The consumed food will be dissolved and be breathed out. How amazing it is that the consumed food is exhaled along with the breath with a pleasant aroma and then it disappears into the air!

In Luke 24:41-43 it is written, *"While they still could not believe it because of their joy and amazement, He said to them, 'Have you anything here to eat?' They gave Him a piece of a broiled fish; and He took it and ate it before them."* The Lord ate before His disciples to let them have the faith of resurrection and to let them know about the resurrected body. It was also to let them know the fact that a spiritual body can also eat. Mary Magdalene and the disciples did not recognize the resurrected Jesus at first. It was because of the light that was coming out from the resurrected body. The resurrected body does not have any scars, but for the doubt of Thomas, Jesus showed him His hands. Jesus let Thomas see the scars but for the moment so that he could gain faith.

The Perfected Heavenly Body

It is explained that those who will have the resurrected body will be caught up into the air for the Seven-year Wedding

Banquet. After that, in that same body, they will come down to this earth during the Millennium Kingdom. When it is over, they will inherit their respective heavenly dwelling place through the Great White Throne Judgment. When this happens, they will be changed into the *perfected heavenly body,* which can be considered as a spiritual body at a level higher than the resurrected body. Now, why did God let us have an interim stage? Why do we receive the resurrected body and not the perfected heavenly body from the start?

It's mainly because the kingdom of heaven that is in the third heaven and the place for Seven-year Wedding Banquet in the second heaven will have many differences including the density of spirit and flow of time. For this reason God gives us the body that is the most suitable for each space. The common factor for the spiritual form, the resurrected body, and the perfected heavenly body is that they all show a different brilliance of aurora-like lights that emanate according to the extent to which one has achieved holiness. In addition to giving out different lights according to the measure of each one's holiness, the perfected heavenly body also shows the reward and glory each person receives from God. This is the biggest difference between the resurrected body and the perfected heavenly body.

When the human cultivation is over, each one's level of sanctification will be finalized, and the amount of rewards will be according to it. Thus, one can distinguish the differences in the glory and rewards seeing the spiritual light of each person. But of course all things will be clearly revealed only after the Great

White Throne Judgment. One will have the perfected heavenly body only after God officially recognizes and proclaims the glory and rewards given to each person.

Light of Glory

The brilliance of the aurora-like light of the spiritual form is different according to the level of holiness each person achieves on this earth. For this reason this brilliance is called the 'light of glory'. The more holiness and resemblance to the Lord one has achieved, the clearer and brighter this light will be. We will also be able to tell the rank in the spiritual order just by seeing the brightness of the light. In particular, those who are in the Second Kingdom of Heaven and those in the Third Kingdom of Heaven will have very different appearances. It's because the light of glory, the clothes they wear, the patterns and decorations on their clothes, and their hair styles will all be different.

Revelation 19:8 says, *"It was given to her to clothe herself in fine linen, bright and clean; for the fine linen is the righteous acts of the saints."* As said, both men and women wear bright white fine linen in Heaven.

The clothes are as soft as silk and they flutter for they are very light. There is no dust and people do not sweat, so the clothes never get dirty even though they are worn for a long time. There are many kinds of adornments and different patterns, which make them very splendid and beautiful beyond comparison with any dress on this earth. Furthermore, rainbow colors and other various colors of lights emanate from the clothes.

There are clothes for everyday use, party dresses, clothing for worship services, sports-wear, and even clothing for playing various games. They can have appropriate outfits according to each occasion. In Heaven, people receive rewards according to their deeds on this earth. So, each one receives different kinds and numbers of clothes. Some of them have just several while others may have countless numbers of various kinds of clothing. Of course, recognizing the glory is not just about clothes. We can also recognize each one's glory and rewards through their crowns worn on their heads and other decorations.

The number, the kinds, the light, and splendor of the crowns given will be different according to the extent to which we cultivate holiness and work faithfully for the kingdom of God with faith. The density, the scheme, and the clarity of the brilliance of the colors are different in each heavenly dwelling place. But even the clothes in the lowest level dwelling place in Heaven will be much more splendid, beautiful, and clearer in color than any clothes of this earth. The perfected heavenly body itself is so beautiful that it wouldn't need any additional decoration or ornamentation, but God gives the clothes, crowns, and other accessories according to each one's deeds.

2. Soul and Body Belonging to Spirit

The saved children of God will live in Heaven in the perfected heavenly body after the Great White Throne Judgment. The perfected heavenly body has the soul that obeys the spirit and a spiritual body that does not produce any kind of body waste.

Why is it important to understand about spirit, soul, and body? It is because we have to recover the spirit and soul and the body that have been changed due to the sin of Adam. This is also the reason why God cultivates human beings on this earth. When we accept Jesus Christ and receive the Holy Spirit, our dead spirit is revived, and then we have to recover our spirit. To the extent that we recover our spirit, we will have the soul and the body that belong to the spirit. We can then be people who belong to spirit.

When one has soul and body that belong to spirit, this is said to be the state where the 'soul is prosperous'. It is recorded in 3 John 1:2 that says, *"Beloved, I pray that in all respects you may prosper and be in good health, just as your soul prospers."*

Once one's soul prospers, a person can cut out the thoughts belonging to flesh. If they want to stop thinking about something, it can be done immediately. A person can stop smelling and hearing certain things. The sensation of pain can be sensed or not as one desires. Since thoughts and feelings can be controlled at will, there is always a fullness of joy and thanks (Romans 8:6). Such a person is healthy and all things go well with him. Diseases cannot affect him because he can control his body, too. Even if he gets an illness due to his mistake, he can overcome it immediately with faith.

Soul Belonging to Spirit

Adam, the first man that God created, was a living spirit, and he had a spirit, a soul, and a body that belonged to spirit. His spirit was his master. It controlled his soul and body in truth. But from the time he sinned and his spirit died, his spirit, soul, and body came to belong to flesh. When man was a living spirit, he was supplied with only truth from God, and thus he had the operations of soul belonging to only spirit. But Satan came into control of the soul of man since man's spirit died. With a dead spirit man could no longer have operations of soul belonging to spirit.

However, after a person accepts Jesus Christ, he can regain operations of soul belonging to spirit to the extent that he gives birth to spirit through the Holy Spirit and obeys the Word of God. His faulty knowledge and theories and his thoughts that are not pleasing in God's sight will be changed into the truth. It is as written in 2 Corinthians 10:5, *"We are destroying speculations and every lofty thing raised up against the knowledge of God, and we are taking every thought captive to the obedience of Christ."*

Men naturally receive the works of Satan to the extent that they have soul belonging to flesh. Even if they try to have operations of soul belonging to spirit they cannot do it as they wish. Therefore, they have to keep on trying to change their operations of soul into those belonging to truth by checking their thoughts, words, and actions all the time. As they continuously try with fervent prayers, they will be able to gain operations of soul belonging to spirit through the grace and power of God and the help of the Holy Spirit.

The soul that belongs to spirit obeys spirit, because spirit, which is the original master of man, performs its role as the master. Then, this person will have only thoughts of goodness, love, and truth for he has only operations of soul belonging to spirit. For example, even if others act in rudeness or do something evil to him, a person who has the soul belonging to spirit won't have his feelings hurt. He desires peace and understands others without any form of confrontation with them. Rather than having aggravated feelings, he has sympathy for others for having evil in them.

Of course, even for those people whose souls prosper, they still have untruths that were input in their memory. But, even though the memory is there, Satan cannot work on it once the untruths are cast off from the heart. Naturally, they have only operations of soul belonging to spirit. They follow the guidance of the Holy Spirit, so they do not see the things they are not supposed to see. They do not pass any judgment or condemnation, and they live according to the truth.

If they continue to have the operations of soul belonging to spirit, the operation of soul belonging to flesh itself can disappear completely. They come to hate seeing, hearing, or speaking anything that is of untruth. This means the vessel of their hearts is filled fully with truth. Because untruths have been completely removed from their hearts, untruths will also disappear from their thoughts, too. This way, if we fill our hearts only with truth and fill it completely, we will only have soul belonging to truth.

The Soul Knows All But Only Thinks Truth

When we go to Heaven later, it is not just our spirit that goes to Heaven. Our soul will also be accommodated in the spiritual form. This soul is the soul that belongs to spirit, namely the truth. Only the portion of our soul from which the untruth has been cast out and that has been cultivated as truth will combine with spirit. Does this mean that we will not know anything about the untruth when we are in Heaven? No, it doesn't. We will know about untruth and in much more detail than we do now.

1 Corinthians 13:12 says, *"For now we see in a mirror dimly, but then face to face; now I know in part, but then I will know fully just as I also have been fully known."* The mirrors used about 2,000 years ago were polished plates of silver, bronze, or steel, and they were dim compared to modern mirrors. They could see the general figures of things, but things were not clear in the mirror. But today's mirrors are very clear. It is the same in Heaven. We will know everything clearly and exactly, even the things that we did not know here on this earth.

As long as we have souls belonging to spirit, even though we think about some things that brought shame or humiliation to us on this earth, we will not have any thoughts of untruth or hard feelings about them. We will just have thoughts of spirit and thoughts of truth in gentleness, peace, and mercy.

Understanding Each Other's Heart in Spirit

Other people's hearts can be felt and correctly discerned in Heaven, and we will be able to understand and sense the feelings of others. They do not have any evil in their hearts, either, and thus, there are no misunderstandings and there is no prejudice or judging. Especially in New Jerusalem, they understand each other's heart completely in spirit. Each word they say will contain consideration, love, and service thereby touching others' hearts. They understand the heart of God the Father and the Lord as well as other people's hearts, so they will understand what kind of mind and feelings God had while they were going through human cultivation on the Earth; they will also understand what kinds of feelings the Lord had when He was taking the cross.

Once through inspiration, God let me feel the heart of Moses. I met Moses standing in such bright lights, and he was filled with the aroma of goodness. When he held my hands, God's love was delivered to me. When he opened his mouth to speak, he had the boldness and dignity that he had when he was delivering the Word of God to the sons of Israel in the wilderness.

Moses let me know the things about his childhood in the palace of Egypt. He let me know how he came to learn about God the Almighty and that he was a Hebrew through his nanny who was actually his mother. He let me know about the occasion in which the sons of Israel worshiped idols in the wilderness and what kinds of feelings and emotions he had as the leader of the Exodus. Moses had tears that welled up remembering those moments.

When somebody sheds tears remembering the things that happened on this earth, those tears will soon be changed into beautiful lights. Those who are listening to what is said will also feel the goodness and love for the souls which will move the heart.

They will once again become thankful for the love of God who has given them the happiness in Heaven and give glory to Him from their heart. They love God with all their heart, mind, and soul, and their love and thanks never change. They deeply understand the providence of God, which is that He wants to gain true children to share His love with Him, even though it means He has to go through so many painful things in the process of human cultivation. That is why they will be grateful forever from the depth of their heart.

The Body Belonging to Spirit

Like the living spirit, Adam was not perfect, spirit that does not know about flesh is not perfect. In the same way, flesh that does not know spirit has no value. All those who do not accept Jesus Christ as their personal savior are all men of flesh. As such they cannot really know about God's kingdom and the spiritual realm. They will eventually suffer agony in the eternal fire of Hell. So, what is their worth going to be? Only those who know both fleshly realm and spiritual realm, and cast away flesh to go into spirit have value as men.

To the extent that we cultivate holiness in our hearts, our flesh will also change into that which belongs to spirit. Those who were weak and sickly will become healthy to the same extent that they are changed into spirit even though they are not yet completely sanctified.

Once we go into spirit, our spirit will embrace the soul and body so that they will move together as one entity. Even though we are living in this physical space, we control our soul and body through spirit, so it is the same as though we were living in spiritual space. To the extent that we recover the image of God that was lost due to Adam's sin, we can clearly communicate with God and receive blessings and all things will go well with us.

Also, once we become men of spirit, our aging will slow down, and furthermore if we go into whole spirit, we can be rejuvenated. In Moses' case, his eyes were not dim and his strength did not weaken until he died at the age of 120. Abraham begot Isaac though he was too old to have a son. Moreover, forty years after Isaac was born, he fathered six more children (Genesis

25). In case of Elijah and Enoch, they cast off all forms of flesh and went into such deep levels of spirit that they showed the characters of God. For this reason they were no longer under the law of the spiritual realm that says the wages of sin is death, and thus they were able to avoid death.

The Body That Doesn't Need Food

When God's children enter into the heavenly kingdom they will eventually have the perfected heavenly body. Their bodies do not perish or decay and they will enjoy eternal life. Matthew 26:29 says, *"But I say to you, I will not drink of this fruit of the vine from now on until that day when I drink it new with you in My Father's kingdom."*

The resurrected Lord will not eat anything until He will eat with the saved believers after human cultivation comes to an end. Just like the resurrected Lord, we do not have to eat to continue our lives once we have a spiritual body.

But the aroma and elements contained in the food in Heaven have good effects on the spiritual form, so they can eat or breathe in the aroma. They can breathe in the aroma of flowers or fruits, and they can do it not just with the nose, but also through the whole body and through the heart. When people once offered sacrifices of animals in the times of the Old Testament, God smelled the aroma of the heart that came from the people who were giving the sacrifices. Even today, when we offer up worship services, praises and offerings, God accepts the aroma of our hearts.

By breathing in the aroma greater joy and happiness of Heaven is felt. Even on this earth, we feel happier when we eat various kinds of foods. Similarly, spiritual bodies take delight in breathing in aromas. In Heaven, nobody gets tired of anything, and they can feel the same happiness and satisfaction even though they breathe in the same aroma all the time. When they breathe in the scents of the fruits and flowers, they are absorbed in the body for a little while and then given off to the air. People's hearts will be filled with more happiness in this process.

There is No Bodily Waste

The perfected heavenly body is a body. It can smell and eat food. It can eat various fruits and drink various kinds of drinks made with the water of life. In addition to the twelve fruits from the tree of life, there are so many other kinds of fruits in Heaven, and we can eat as much and as many fruits as we want. There are also many kinds of drinks.

In Heaven, would we also eat the foods that we liked on this earth? Would there be meat, bread, and cakes in Heaven? Would we miss some foods of this earth? Once we go to Heaven, we would not want to eat any food that we used to have on this earth. Once we have a body that is the most suitable for the space of the third heaven, we can live forever even without eating.

Of course, you might remember a particular kind of food you enjoyed on this earth and would like to eat something similar in Heaven. You might then make something that is similar to it. But since the fruits and drinks of Heaven taste much better, you wouldn't want to enjoy any kind of physical food of the past.

When we eat something in Heaven, it will be dissolved and emitted during respiration, so there will be no form of excretion as on earth. The food consumed will be given off naturally with the breath, stay as fragrance for a while, and disappear into the air. How convenient and amazing it is that we wouldn't have to digest or excrete like on this earth! Obviously there will not be bathroom that might have any objectionable odors. In Heaven, we will have this perfected heavenly body.

This is the same in any dwelling place of the kingdom of heaven. But if we have more of the soul belonging to flesh and less of the soul belonging to spirit, the brilliance of the spiritual form will be weak. According to the extent to which we cultivate our soul to belong to spirit, we will be given a dwelling pace in Paradise, the First Kingdom of Heaven, or the Second Kingdom of Heaven. We can enter into the Third Kingdom of Heaven or New Jerusalem only when we make our soul belong to spirit completely without any part of soul that belongs to flesh.

God lets us reap what we sow and gives us back as we have acted in His love and justice. The heavenly dwelling place and the heavenly rank will be decided according to the brightness of our spiritual light, and therefore, we should strive with fervent prayers to become a man who has spirit, soul, and body that belong to spirit.

3. God's Gift

God has prepared a gift for the saved children, and it is the eternal life in the heavenly kingdom. We will receive a different heavenly dwelling place according to how we go through human cultivation on this earth to become a person who seeks after God's heart.

The grand project of God to harvest believers who are the 'wheat' of the harvest is still going on today. He is looking for those who believe in the power and divine nature of God that are seen in all things in nature and who live by the Word of God. They are souls that are as clear and beautiful as crystal. The Bible tells us about the end of days. Those who are spiritually awake feel that the end of human cultivation is very near.

Since the fall of Adam, mankind produced offspring and developed civilizations. They also experienced life, aging, illness, and death. After human cultivation is over, God will invite all the believers to enter into the 'air' which is located in the second heaven. He will throw an 'entrancing' wedding banquet and let us share our love with the Lord for seven years.

Revelation 19:7-9 describes it:

Let us rejoice and be glad and give the glory to Him, for the marriage of the Lamb has come and His bride has made herself ready. It was given to her to clothe herself in fine linen, bright and clean; for the fine linen is the righteous acts of the saints. Then he said to

107

me, "Write, 'Blessed are those who are invited to the marriage supper of the Lamb.'" And he said to me, "These are true words of God."

God's love does not end here. After the wedding banquet is over, just as a newly wedded couple go on a honeymoon after the wedding banquet, God will let us go down to this earth with the Lord and reign with Him for a thousand years. He will renew the first heaven, which was the stage of human cultivation, and let the saved believers share their love with the Lord to the fullest extent.

Revelation 20:6 says, *"Blessed and holy is the one who has a part in the first resurrection; over these the second death has no power, but they will be priests of God and of Christ and will reign with Him for a thousand years."*

God will reveal the gifts and rewards that He has prepared for His beloved children after the Millennium Kingdom is over. In the Great White Throne Judgment, He will give rewards for what they did while on this earth and He will assign their dwelling place in Heaven according to each one's measure of faith. They are given permanent dwelling places in the third heaven, which is a place free of tears, sorrow, pains, diseases, and death, so that they can live a life filled with goodness, love, joy, and happiness in the perfected heavenly body.

Jesus promises in John 14:2-3, *"In My Father's house are many dwelling places; if it were not so, I would have told you; for I go to prepare a place for you. If I go and prepare a place for you, I will come again and receive you to Myself, that where I am, there you may be also.''*

What does the eternal kingdom of heaven look like, and what kind of life are we going to live there?

New Heaven and New Earth

The sky in Heaven is a clean and clear blue. The reason why God made the color of the sky blue is because it lets us feel depth, height, and clarity. He wants His beloved children to live happily forever having clear and beautiful hearts like crystal.

There are also clouds in the sky of the heavenly kingdom. The clouds are a form of decoration to increase the beauty. The clouds add happiness to the hearts of heavenly citizens. When those who are in New Jerusalem think of and praise the love of God looking up into the sky, angels read the minds of their masters and sometimes make heart-shaped clouds or write things using the clouds.

In Heaven, there is the light of the glory of God, which cannot even be compared with the sunlight. It shines every corner brightly beginning from New Jerusalem to Paradise (Revelation 22:5).

The light of the glory of God is so clear and bright that if it were to shine about those who are in Paradise, they would not even be able to lift up their heads because of its brilliance. For this reason, God increasingly diminishes the brightness of the light in other dwelling places from that of New Jerusalem. As you move further from New Jerusalem and the Third Kingdom of Heaven into the Second Kingdom of Heaven, the First Kingdom of Heaven, and Paradise, the brilliance of the light diminishes.

By the power of God there are the four seasons—spring, summer, autumn, and winter—in Heaven. They do not actually need four seasons, but they are prepared for the children of God so that they can enjoy the different natural appearance of each season. They can see the leaves of autumn and even snow of winter.

God has made the things in a most perfect and beautiful way so that we can feel the beauty we had in the different seasons on this earth. But it does not mean that in Heaven there will be 'cold' or 'hot' associated with weather and the seasons. There are distinctions of different seasons but it won't be marked by either hotness or coldness of the seasons. The temperature will be the most suitable to live all the time.

The soil of Heaven is not made of dust but of gold, silver, and different gemstones. Steel has a moderate density on earth but when it is powdered, it is blown by the wind. But if it's in the shape of a ball, it will not be blown by the wind. The gold, silver, and other precious gemstones are in spherical shapes, so there is no dust in Heaven.

The Golden Road and the Jewel Road

In every dwelling place of Heaven, there is a golden road. Of course, the glitter that comes out from the golden road is different from place to place in Heaven. The closer you get to New Jerusalem, the brighter the glitter's brilliance becomes. Unlike the pure gold of this earth, the gold in Heaven is hard, but it feels very soft when you walk on it. On this earth a piece of gold as large as a man's hand is quite rare. But, when you see the endless golden road that shines like glass, can you imagine just how magnificent it will be! Pure gold stands for the unchanging quality of spiritual faith. The brilliance of the glitter of the golden road in each dwelling place is different because the heavenly dwelling place will be determined by each one's measure of faith.

God does not ascribe much meaning in the gold of Paradise. However, as you move from the First Kingdom of Heaven to the Second Kingdom of Heaven and the Third Kingdom of Heaven, the residents will be closer to the perfect measure of faith, so the pure gold in each of the higher dwelling places will have a deeper meaning which will be revealed by the brilliance of the glitter.

In addition to the golden road, there are other kinds of roads like the flower road and jewel road. There are also some roads where you will be transported by the power of God just by standing on it. The spiritual form is very light, as if it does not have any weight. So if you walk on flowers, the flowers are not damaged. The flowers rejoice and give out more fragrance when the children of God approach them.

The jewel roads have many kinds of gemstones that emanate wonderful lights. If you step on them, they give out even more beautiful lights. But the jewel roads cannot be seen everywhere in the heavenly kingdom. They are constructed only in and around the houses of those who resemble the Lord completely and have made great contributions to fulfilling God's providence of human cultivation.

The River of Water of Life

The River of the Water of Life originates from the throne of God. It flows all throughout the heavenly kingdom and returns to its origin. This river is as clear and pure as crystal, and it flows very quietly as if it were not flowing at all. It never evaporates or becomes polluted. It is like the waves of the sea that shine like jewels reflecting the sunshine on a clear day. It represents the heart of God who is the source of the water of life that revives all things in nature. God's heart is a beautiful heart that is dazzlingly brilliant and free of blemish and spot. It is perfect in everything.

The fact that the river of water of life flows all throughout the heavenly kingdom, has the meaning that God rules over all the souls in Heaven, letting them live a joyous life every day by His grace. The taste of the water of life is somewhat sweet and is something we can never taste on this earth. It gives us life, strength, and happiness as we drink it.

Revelation 22:2 says that it flows in the middle of the street. So, on both the sides of the river are the roads. It originates from the throne of God and flows through all corners of the heavenly kingdom, so if you walk on the road on either side of the river, you will eventually reach God's throne. This fact spiritually signifies that if we live by the Word of God, which is represented by the water of life, we will not only reach the heavenly kingdom but also we will reach the most beautiful dwelling place of Heaven, New Jerusalem.

In between the river of water of life and the road on either side are the river banks that have golden and silvery sands. Though hard, the ball-shaped sands in Heaven feel soft. People cannot be injured if they roll or run on it and they won't be scratched by it. The sand does not get blown away and it does not stick like dust to heavenly attire.

You can swim in the river, too. Even though you do not know how to swim on this earth, you can swim freely in Heaven. To go swimming on this earth we usually have to change into swimming suits. But the water in Heaven does not permeate the clothing of Heaven. It just rolls off the surface of the clothing's materials. So you can swim freely wearing your ordinary clothing.

There are beautiful benches that are built on the golden roads that stretch out on either side of the river. Around them are twelve different kinds of fruits from the tree of life. Revelation 22:2 says, *"On either side of the river was the tree of life, bearing twelve kinds of fruit, yielding its fruit every month..."* This does not mean a fruit will fall and then another fruit will replace it every month. It means the twelve kinds of fruits are always there.

The fruit of life is as big as a melon, but has a shape similar to an apple. It is reddish, and the color is beautiful. The twelve fruits are slightly different in their luster, size, shape, and taste. If somebody picks one of the fruit, a new fruit will grow immediately to replace it. It is more fragrant than any fruit of this earth and the taste is beyond human words. It melts in your mouth like cotton candy.

In a vision God once showed to me a scene of the river of water of life. The children of God were sitting on benches that were decorated with gold and precious gemstones. They were having pleasant conversations with each other. If they harbored the thought that they wanted to eat the fruit of life during their conversation, the ministering angels would read their mind and bring the fruits in a golden basket. You can look at the river while sitting on the benches with the beloved around you or you can have a pleasant dialogue with them while just walking. How happy such a life will be!

Animals and Plants of Heaven

In Heaven, the number of kinds of animals, birds, and fish is simply innumerable. There are some kinds that are not on this earth and there are those that are present on this earth but are not found in Heaven. Those animals that are deemed detestable in Leviticus 11 are not found in Heaven.

The animals in Heaven are slightly bigger than those of this earth. They seem to be a little statelier and yet they are mild in temperament and they are obedient. The fur of mammals and feathers of birds give out brilliant lights and gentle fragrance. Even the lion is not ferocious but mild. The clean fur and golden mane are wonderfully amazing to behold.

The animals in Heaven welcome God's children and rejoice when they see them. Especially in New Jerusalem, there will be some people who will receive animals as personal pets or even a zoo as their rewards. The animals perform cute tricks to please their master. It is not that they understand the mind of their masters because they have soul. It is just as angels obey the commands of God, the animals in Heaven, being spiritual beings, almost automatically act in a way to be loved by their masters.

In Heaven, there are many kinds of plants including the tree of life, other fruit trees, and flowers. The plants on this earth gain nutrients from the roots and through the process of photosynthesis to produce an energy source. But plants in Heaven live forever without these processes, but with the power of life given by God. The roots of the plants do not absorb nutrients. They just reveal the characteristics of each plant. Of course, the shapes of flowers, their scents, and fruits can show the distinction, but the roots are also a means to show such differences.

Plants in Heaven give out their unique scent strongly yet gently. They may shake or bend their branches to express a certain meaning. They can move as if they were angels dancing to praise songs. They might also praise God by giving out their fragrance as much as they can.

The leaves, flowers, or fruits never fall even with the passage of time. Their aroma and colors never change. If you pluck a flower, a new flower will replace it immediately. So is the case with fruits. The flowers that are picked also do not wither and their freshness is maintained. If you want to keep the flower, it will last as long as you would like it to. If you want to dispose of it, it will just be dissolved and then disappear into the air. Some flowers give out stronger scents when they are powdered. If you want to, you can keep it in a bottle as long as you want.

Each plant has its own unique scent. They have a fresh, sweet, gentle or noble scent. The fragrance in each heavenly dwelling place has different meanings. For example, the roses in Paradise are just one of the many flowers there. But in the house of an individual in New Jerusalem, the heart of the owner will be contained in the fragrance of the rose in the home. When there is a guest visiting, the roses will give out the particular aroma to the guest to express the heart of the owner. The roses in different houses in New Jerusalem will give out different kinds of fragrance.

Also, some of the plants that are in New Jerusalem are not present in other dwelling places. The number of kinds of flowers decreases as you go down from New Jerusalem to Paradise. Also, the freedom to personally use the flowers is increasingly limited. The comfort of sitting on the grass lawn and the color of the lawn are different in each dwelling place as well.

Everything in Heaven, including animals and plants, is prepared by God for His saved children. To those true children of God who lived only by the will of God on this earth will be given everything they want in Heaven.

Cultural Life in Heaven

God has made a variety of recreational facilities in each heavenly dwelling place to give His children greater joy and happiness. They are incomparably larger than the biggest amusement parks of this world. They have so many exciting things too.

Since we are in the perfected heavenly body in Heaven, there is no need of fear. You would not be afraid of any of the rides such as roller coasters. You will just be thrilled by them. Besides the amusement parks, there are so many other things for entertainment, recreation and enjoyment. We can also have hobbies to improve talents in certain skills in Heaven just like we do on this earth.

We can enjoy the things that we used to enjoy on this earth. Moreover, if there are things that we restrained ourselves from doing on this earth to accomplish more of God's work, we will enjoy them as much as we want. We will also learn new things. For example, we can learn to play musical instruments such as violin, flute, or harp. In Heaven, everyone is wise and excellent, so we can learn how to play them very quickly.

The sports in Heaven exclude any game that can cause injury or harm to others. There will be certain rules for each game too. We can have team sports such as volleyball, basketball, soccer, or baseball. There will also be more individual games such as tennis, skiing, golf, bowling, and swimming. We can also enjoy such sports as hang gliding, wind surfing, or sail-boating. The sports facilities and equipment in Heaven are accident-free and are decorated with gold and jewels to add to our joy.

Heaven is not a place where you get pleasure by winning in competition. You can get enough pleasure and satisfaction just by the fact that you can play at the sports. What is the meaning of games that do not have winners, you might ask? But because there is no evil in Heaven, to give more pleasure and benefit to others is to win the game.

Of course, there are also games from which you can get pleasure by competition in good faith. For example, people breathe in fragrance of the flowers as much as they can and breathe it out in front of other people. The scores will be given according to the magnitude to which you please God by breathing out fragrance, or according to how well you blend many kinds of aromas. It is a competition about how much pleasure you can give to other people, and this is also pleasing in God's sight. There are also so many other kinds of entertainment in Heaven that have more fun than anything on this earth. They don't cause tiredness like arcade games or video games, and you never get bored of anything.

You can also watch movies in Heaven. In the theaters, you can see some monumental events that happened during the course of human cultivation. The Creation, Noah's flood, the Exodus, Jesus' ministry, the providence of cross, the fiery works of the Holy Spirit at the end time, and the stories of each of the fathers of faith will all be made into movies.

For example, you can watch a movie about the whole life of the apostle Paul. You can watch how he met the Lord and how he dedicated his whole life with his love for the Lord. You can learn the detailed things that are not recorded in the Bible. You will see Paul's life as if you were with him in person in such events as his being persecuted so severely—beyond the measures of human endurance. You can experience his imprisonment in Philippi, and the giving of thanks to God and praising Him even while being in the sea after being shipwrecked. How emotionally riveting it will be!

Transportation in Heaven

We can visit mysterious and beautiful places in the heavenly kingdom. There will be unique, breathtaking scenes wherever we go. Being in the perfected heavenly body, there is no tiring even after traveling for a long time. The heart of spirit is never changing, so we never get bored even if we visit the same place.

There will be different means of transport for traveling. There are public forms of transportation such as heavenly train. There is privately-owned transportation such as cloud automobiles or the golden wagon. The heavenly train is decorated with brilliant jewels in different colors, and it provides the passengers with the greatest comfort. It will be really delightful to see the scenes outside the windows, too. When believers in Paradise are invited to visit New Jerusalem, they will go by heavenly train. The train actually can fly in the sky at a very high speed.

Though it is called a cloud automobile, it is not made of vapor, but of the cloud of glory. It adds to the beauty of heavenly life. When you ride the cloud automobile, it makes others sense dignity and authority. When the Lord comes back again, He will come in clouds (1 Thessalonians 4:16-17; Revelation 1:7). It is because it will look more dignified, honorable, and beautiful to come in the clouds of glory.

God gives the cloud automobile to those who go to the Third Kingdom of Heaven or higher. In the Third Kingdom of Heaven, the automobiles are for public use, but in New Jerusalem, they are given for private use. In this sense, possessing the cloud automobile itself shows the glory of the owner.

Those who are in New Jerusalem can also go on a trip with the Lord in cloud automobiles. The cloud automobiles are usually driven by angels. Some of them are like small passenger cars while others are bigger and have many seats for more passengers. The designs, colors, and decorations also vary. There is also an automobile made of a little piece of cloud. It is used for short distances. It takes a person and drops him gently at the destination, for example like a golf cart when he is golfing!

Worship Service and Education in Heaven

We will attend worship services in Heaven, too. God Himself will deliver the messages. We will learn about the spiritual realm in detail including the origin of God, the Beginning of Time, and eternity. We will also have time to listen to the Lord. We will also talk with God, the Lord, and the Holy Spirit, and this is the prayer in Heaven. We will also praise God with new songs.

In Heaven, if you have to visit a place that is at a higher level than your dwelling place, you have to change your clothes to those that are in accordance with the place and occasion. The worship service held in New Jerusalem will be broadcast everywhere, so everyone can attend the service anywhere in Heaven. But complicated equipment is not necessary for this. The angels will unfold something like an immense piece of cloth, which will become the video screen. The lights and colors will be automatically adjusted for each dwelling place, so that they can watch the vivid video that makes them feel as if they were in the actual place.

The reason why the lights have to be adjusted in each dwelling place is that, if the lights of God are relayed as they are, those who are in the Third Kingdom of Heaven or below cannot directly see Him because the lights are far too brilliant. Those who are in the Second Kingdom and below would not be able to even lift up their heads to look at the face of our Father God on screen, because their consciences will not allow them to do it.

It is particularly so for those who are in Paradise who received

121

'salvation with shame'. They cannot even look at the video screen due to embarrassment and somewhat shameful feelings. In addition to the worship services where God is the speaker, you can invite the Lord, the Holy Spirit, or the fathers of faith such as Moses and Paul to speak at worship services.

We will continue to learn new things even after we get to Heaven. The kingdom of heaven is endless, and therefore no matter how much we study we can never learn everything about God the Creator who exists from before eternity and throughout all eternity. It is difficult to fully understand the endless depth of God who rules over everything in the universe. We will feel that Heaven is filled with things that we truly have to learn. But the learning in Heaven, unlike on this earth, will only be joyous. We will understand everything as we learn it. We will never forget what we once understood so there is nothing difficult about learning. Moreover, we do not just listen to lectures. There will be three-dimensional programs that help our understanding.

Imagine the original voice of God saying "Let there be light" that is sounding all throughout the universe, the light being formed, and also the lights being separated, and all these scenes are occurring right in front of your eyes! Also, imagine you can see the expanse being formed from the water and the water being divided from the water. How grand and magnificent it will be!

Various Banquets in Heaven

Various banquets in Heaven can be considered the

culmination of the joy of heavenly life. They let us feel the abundance, freedom, beauty, and glory of Heaven at a glance. In banquets people will watch special performances or dance with their beloved ones in the most beautiful outfits and decorations they have. Even though you do not dance well on this earth, you can learn it quickly and dance well in Heaven.

Even on this earth, one being full of the inspiration of the Holy Spirit might go into a state where new tongues and new songs come out. Then the hands and arms will move automatically in rhythm to dance and praise God. In Heaven, with the perfected heavenly body, anybody can dance beautifully to any kind of music. One can even give glory to God with a solo dance.

There are many kinds of feasts in Heaven, and the sizes and levels are different in each dwelling place. In New Jerusalem, there are banquets held in the name of God the Trinity, or banquets held in the name of God the Father, God the Son, and God the Holy Spirit respectively. At times all the people in all the heavenly dwelling places will be invited to participate in the banquet that is given in the name of God the Trinity.

For example, after the Great White Throne Judgment, we are given our respective dwelling places in Heaven, and then there will be the first banquet held in New Jerusalem. God will invite all citizens of the heavenly kingdom to this banquet. All those who are in New Jerusalem and the Third Kingdom of Heaven can attend it, but from the Second Kingdom of Heaven, to the First Kingdom of Heaven, and Paradise, only the representatives can actually come to the banquet.

When people from other dwelling places come to a banquet held in New Jerusalem, they have to change their clothes and decorations so that they are befitting New Jerusalem. It is because the light of the heavenly bodies is different in each dwelling place. Once they put on the clothes that are suitable in New Jerusalem, they can adapt themselves to the place, and they will be suitable for the banquet held there.

There are designated areas where people can change their outfits. There are so many kinds of clothes prepared for them. The angels help them change the attire as it is selected. But those who are from Paradise have to change by themselves without the help of the angels. Once they wear the radiant clothes of New Jerusalem, they will be moved by the inexpressible glory, and they will feel undeserving because it is attire that they did not earn the privilege to wear.

Unlike the clothes, the crowns are not prepared for in New Jerusalem. Each one has to bring his own crown. The crowns in the Third Kingdom of Heaven are very different from those in New Jerusalem, and there is a small, round mark on the right corner of the crown. Those who are from the Second Kingdom of Heaven, the First Kingdom of Heaven, and Paradise put a round symbol on their left chest so they will be easily distinguished from those who are in New Jerusalem or the Third Kingdom of Heaven. Those from the Second and First Kingdoms of Heaven put on their crowns to attend the banquet, but those from Paradise do not have crowns and they do not wear one.

Banquets of Different Dwelling Places

The angels usually take care of the decorations, ushering, food service, and all other aspects for preparation of the heavenly feasts. Just as airplanes have different services according to the class of travel, the level of service and all the preparations of the banquets are different in each heavenly dwelling place.

If we say the banquets of New Jerusalem are feasts given by the royal or noble family, then the banquets in Paradise can be likened to a party that poor peasants have with their neighbors. But this is just an allegory, and it does not mean the banquets in Paradise are somewhat shabby and poorly prepared. It just means that there is such a great difference between the banquets in New Jerusalem and those in Paradise.

The banquets in Paradise are not given by any individual. They are for the general public or certain groups. There are no ministering angels, so the people have to prepare everything by themselves. But even in Paradise, there is no evil but only goodness and love, so everyone will prepare for them with joy and happiness. Everyone serves each other with consideration, so they can enjoy the most out of it. In fact, it is a kind of happiness that we can never feel even at the most luxurious party of this world. So, how great the happiness and bliss of banquets in New Jerusalem are going to be!

Performances

Songs and dances are vital parts of banquets in Heaven as well as on this earth. Beautiful angels dance elegantly or play musical instruments and sing songs. There are also performers who praise or play instruments along with the angels. The praising, dance, and instrumentals performed by angels are spotlessly beautiful and skillful. But God accepts something more pleasingly than the performances of angels. They are praising, dances, and instrumental performances of God's children because they offer them with an understanding of God's heart and with their love for Him.

There are special kinds of performing halls in New Jerusalem, too. There are grand and marvelous halls that are much bigger and more beautiful than Carnegie Hall or Madison Square Garden in New York City, or the Opera House in Sydney which constantly host performances. It is not for the performers to show off their skills. It is only to give glory to God and render joy and happiness to the Lord and other people.

Mostly, the performers are usually those who have been performers on this earth, and sometimes they reenact what they performed on this earth. Also, there are people who wanted to participate in performances on this earth but could not, and they learn new praise songs and dances in Heaven and present them.

According to the extent to which the performers have become sanctified, they may perform exclusively in New Jerusalem, the Third Kingdom of Heaven, the Second Kingdom of Heaven, or the First Kingdom of Heaven. The singers, dancers, and players of musical instruments for New Jerusalem are the top class performers who are loved by all the people in Heaven. Everyone in Heaven can see their performances because the banquets or the performances held in New Jerusalem in the name of God the Trinity are broadcast live to all heavenly dwelling places.

The video screen will be unfolded in the air at the most comfortable height for their eyes to see, so seeing the vivid video they will feel as if they were in the actual place. In this way the people in other heavenly dwelling places can be touched by the banquets or the performances held in New Jerusalem. Just as celebrities are followed by many fans on this earth, there are angels that are in charge of praising following them. They call them 'Master' and they try to please and give happiness and joy to their masters.

Being loved and adored by countless angels

There is a woman in New Jerusalem who enjoys such great honor and who is followed by countless angels. She is the one who cultivated a perfect heart of spirit on this earth. She is Mary Magdalene. She wears a resplendent dress that comes down to the floor. She has hair that comes down to her waist. She is dazzlingly beautiful with her crown on her head.

Mary Magdalene cultivated perfect goodness while living on this earth, and her spiritual form gives out such a bright light of glory. Her voice is filled with humbleness and is as soft as the sound of the flowing of little stream. When she speaks, the aroma of her humbleness and goodness is delivered, and all the angels and people will be moved by her words. So, sometimes angels around Mary Magdalene circle her around and praise her aroma of goodness.

She is in such an honored position to be able to see God all the time, so one can feel the heart, dignity, and the light of the glory of God just by seeing her. Now, how could Mary Magdalene get to such an honorable position?

Mary Magdalene was healed of many diseases and was set free from the power of darkness by meeting the Lord. She was ever thankful for this grace of the Lord and served Him without changing her attitude. When Jesus was crucified, so many people who used to follow Him left. But she had such an unchanging heart that she was with Jesus until His death. She even visited His tomb. Eventually she came to stay close to the throne of God in New Jerusalem.

God wants to share His eternal love with and receive praises from His true children who have cultivated such a beautiful heart of goodness like Mary Magdalene.

Isaiah 43:21 says, *"The people whom I formed for Myself Will declare My praise."* What God wants is not just beautiful voices, wonderful choreography, or amazing sound of musical instruments. He wants the praises that are coming from truthful and good hearts. God sometimes sings, too. In beautiful melody and rhyme He sings about the amazing things that His only begotten Son Jesus has done, or extraordinary works manifested by the Holy Spirit.

Nobody can imitate His voice in singing. It is so beautiful that everyone will be totally captivated just by hearing it once. It is also such a loud voice that it can shake the whole world, but not everyone in Heaven will be able to hear it. It can be heard only by those who are close to the throne of God in New Jerusalem. Therefore, it is desired that we attain to the level of whole spirit, praise God in the eternal kingdom of heaven, and reach a glorious position where we can even hear the singing of God.

Part 3

Transcending
Human Limitations

Experiencing the Space of God

Seeing God Who Is Light

"Truly, truly, I say to you, he who believes in Me,
the works that I do, he will do also; a
nd greater works than these he will do;
because I go to the Father."
- John 14:12

Chapter 1
God's Space

Unlike the physical space, the space of God is limitless.
Once we become true children of God,
we can transcend human limitations with the unlimited power of God.
In the space of God, things can be created out of nothing,
the dead can come back to life, and anything that God harbors in
His heart can be done. There is nothing that is impossible in that space.

To Possess the Space of God

Works of Creation Takes Place in God's Space

The Works that Transcend Time and Space

Experiencing Movement through the Spaces

Love that Transcends Justice

Space is an extent or expanse of a surface or three-dimensional area. It can also refer to the infinite extension of the three-dimensional region in which all matter exists. Today, there is also a cyber space that is created by computers. It is open to anybody, but people can make use of it in different measure depending on their knowledge and ability to use computers. In the same way, we can use the space of God and experience amazing things recorded in the Bible to the extent that we understand and utilize the space of God.

Spiritual space is not somewhere at the end of the universe. It is very close to our physical space. Just as we can see outside when we open the window of our homes, we can see the spiritual space if the gate of the spiritual realm opens.

In the Bible, we can read about the resurrected Lord ascending into Heaven in view of many disciples. Acts 1:9 says, *"And after He had said these things, He was lifted up while they were looking on, and a cloud received Him out of their sight."* Jesus went into Heaven by spiritual space that was opened at about the height where clouds were formed. If we understand the spiritual space clearly, we can have the answers to many difficult passages in the Bible. We can also have perfect faith and hope of Heaven.

It seems that all men have no other choice but to live according to their limitations of time and space. But we can overcome such limitations if we become true children of God. Even the evil spirits will not be able to touch us. We will eventually go into the kingdom of heaven located in the third heaven, where even the living spirit Adam could not live. Furthermore, we will also experience the unlimited power of God that is of the fourth heaven. *"Because you are sons, God has sent forth the Spirit of His Son into our hearts, crying, 'Abba! Father!' Therefore you are no longer a slave, but a son; and if a son, then an heir through God"* (Galatians 4:6-7).

Space and Dimension in God's View

As it was mentioned in Part 1 'Vast Space of the Spiritual Realm', after God planned for human cultivation, He divided the one original space into many spaces with different dimensions. Generally, He divided the space into four heavens from the first heaven to the fourth heaven. The first heaven is a tiny portion compared to the original, one space. When God created different spaces with different dimensions, He established a principle among them which dictates that the higher dimension can subdue and rule over lower dimensions, and lower dimensions submit to higher dimensions.

The first heaven, which is the physical universe including the

Earth, the sun and the moon and stars that we see, is the first dimension. It is a physical world, so things change, perish, or die. The second dimension is the space in the second heaven. The second heaven is generally divided into the area of light and the area of darkness. In the area of light is Eden, in which the Garden of Eden is located. Adjacent to Eden is the area of darkness where the evil spirits hold the authority of the air.

The third dimension is the heavenly kingdom, the third heaven. This is the place where the saved children of God will live forever. Centering on the New Jerusalem, which houses the throne of God, there are different dwelling places that are differentiated according to the measure of each one's faith. The fourth dimension is the fourth heaven, and it is the space where the original God existed as light and voice. It is the fourth heaven from which God the Trinity rules over all—the third, second, and first heavens—while showing the works of creation that transcend time and space.

This mysterious four-dimensional space is the space of God. It is where the original God existed and it is such a beautiful place. No one can go to that area but God the Trinity and a few persons who have special permission from God.

The space of God is an endless space where God can make existing things disappear and create things out of nothingness. Substances can exist in any form as liquid, gas, and solid matter. Only those who have proper qualifications can enter this area. Now let us look into this mysterious and wondrous space of God.

God's Heart is the Space of God

The space where God existed before the ages is a spiritual realm invisible to our eyes. It was one big space, and at that time the spiritual realm and the physical world were not divided. God existed as the beautiful and brilliant light containing the chiming voice. He moved all throughout the universe, ruling over everything alone.

The original God harbored the whole universe in His heart. In other words, the whole space of the universe was contained in His heart. Let me give you an illustration to better understand 'harboring a space in heart.' If you remember your hometown, you can picture an image of your hometown, and you might wonder how it looks like now. Or, if you think of somebody whom you love and remember from the time when you were with that person, your mind is already at the place where you were with him/her.

As for God, He can be anywhere in the universe transcending time and space if He just harbors it in His heart. We express this trait of God by saying He is 'omnipresent.' Because of this omnipresence He could harbor all the corners of the universe and rule over everything.

Psalm 68:33 reads, *"To Him who rides upon the highest heavens, which are from ancient times; behold, He speaks forth with His voice, a mighty voice."* 'Riding upon the highest heaven' means that God completely ruled over all the spaces from the first heaven to the fourth heaven. It says His voice is mighty, but this voice is not in the audible range with our ears. Once God speaks forth with the original voice of creation, all things will obey it, and His authority and dignity will shake all heavens.

To Possess the Space of God

God wants His beloved children to possess the space of God and rule over all the spaces, too. But there is a condition to be able to possess this space, for there are rules of love and justice established by God for the human cultivation. Justice is the law and principles. Just as there are many laws for society and traffic rules for driving, there is also the Law of God, and this is the justice of God.

Then, what does it mean by possessing the space? It is to harbor the space in one's heart completely. Of course, harboring the space of God in our heart does not mean we can be omnipresent like God. It just means that extraordinary things can take place by unfolding the space of God in this physical world.

When God divided the spaces, He divided them according to His justice and love which are suitable for each space. As we go up the dimension from the first, second, third, and to fourth heaven, the dimension of justice also becomes broader and deeper. Each heaven is maintained in errorless order. The reason that each space has different dimension of justice is because each heaven has different dimension of love. Love and justice cannot be separated. The deeper the dimension of love becomes, the deeper the dimension of justice, too.

When Jesus forgave the woman who had committed adultery, it was out of love going beyond the level of justice (John 8). When the woman was caught at the scene committing adultery, the people who judged by the justice of the first heaven argued that they had to stone her immediately. But Jesus, having the justice of the fourth heaven said, *"I do not condemn you, either. Go. From now on sin no more"* (John 8:11). It was true love contained in justice.

We can possess the space of God and move freely through all the spaces only when we have the love and justice of God completely. Then we can also understand the rules of the spiritual realm and see through all the things that are happening in this physical world. Jesus having no sin at all died on the cross in place of sinners. Because He had the love going beyond justice, Jesus manifested amazing works of God's power such as healing incurable diseases and calming the wind and waves. He was also able to read the thoughts and minds of people belonging to the first dimension.

Those who are in the first dimension are bound by the limitations of time and physical space. But after we accept Jesus Christ and are born again by the Holy Spirit, we can be freed from such limitations to the extent that we cultivate our heart into the spiritual heart. If we become men of spirit and whole spirit who belong to the third dimension which is spiritual realm, the enemy devil and Satan that belong to the second dimension, will fear us even though we are physically in the first dimension.

Genesis 1:28 says, *"God blessed them; and God said to them, 'Be fruitful and multiply, and fill the earth, and subdue it; and rule over the fish of the sea and over the birds of the sky and over every living thing that moves on the earth.'"* Adam was a living spirit. He was a spiritual being living in the second heaven and he had the authority to rule over everything that is in the first heaven.

In the same way, if we can have the justice and love of God that belong to the fourth heaven, we can manifest the power of God that belongs to the fourth heaven going beyond human limitations. That is why Jesus promised in John 14:12, *"Truly, truly, I say to you, he who believes in Me, the works that I do, he will do also; and greater works than these he will do; because I go to the Father."*

Works of Creation Take Place in God's Space

We can accomplish anything as we wish in the space of God. Above all, there will be works of creation. When God made the heavens and the earth and all things in them, it was the work of creation. Jesus also manifested works of creation for He possessed the space of God. One of the best examples is His first sign in His ministry, which is to make wine out of water.

One day He went to a wedding, and they ran out of wine. The Virgin Mary felt sorry for the host and asked Jesus to help him. At first He seemed to refuse Mary's request. But Mary did not get disappointed but showed her unchanging faith. She knew very well who Jesus was and that He was more than able to make wine out of water. Mary believed she had already received the answer from Jesus and so she told the servants to do whatever Jesus told them.

Jesus saw the faith of Mary and told the servants to fill the water pots. When the servants filled the six water pots, Jesus told them to draw some and take it to the headwaiter. By the time the servants took it to the headwaiter the water had turned into wine. Just by harboring it in heart, the water in the six water pots changed into good wine.

In the space of God such a work of creation can take place just by harboring it in heart. Of course, Jesus showed such work of creation when it was appropriate according to the justice of God and not just any time. This sign was made possible because the perfect faith of Mary was good enough to fulfill the justice of God.

Jesus fed thousands of people with five loaves and two fish, and at another time with seven loaves and two fish. What was the justice of God required for this sign here? *"And Jesus called His disciples to Him, and said, 'I feel compassion for the people, because they have remained with Me now three days and have nothing to eat; and I do not want to send them away hungry, for they might faint on the way'"* (Matthew 15:32).

Thousands of people stayed with Jesus for three consecutive

days longing to hear His messages. They listened to Jesus and rejoiced together when sick people were healed. Their faith in Jesus was perfect at least for that moment. Based on this faith of theirs, Jesus' love was added and it fulfilled the justice of God to make the work of creation possible.

Widow of Zarephath Experienced Work of Creation

A similar work of creation is mentioned in 1 Kings 17, too. When Elijah went to Sidon and met with the widow of Zarephath in obedience to the Word of God, she was poverty-stricken. Due to a long drought, they ran out of food. She had just a handful of flour and a little bit of oil. Elijah told her to bake bread with that last bit of food she had, giving her a word of blessing. *"For thus says the LORD God of Israel, 'The bowl of flour shall not be exhausted, nor shall the jar of oil be empty, until the day that the LORD sends rain on the face of the earth'"* (1 Kings 17:14).

Upon hearing this, the widow of Zarephath did not give an excuse but obeyed it. She was not in a situation to do that if we think with common sense. She was in a situation to die after eating the last bit of food she had, and this man was asking for it. She could have thought he was shameless. But she did not. God moved her heart and let her know that he was a man of God, and she obeyed what he had told her.

What kind of blessing did she receive as a result? 1 Kings 17:15-16 says, *"So she went and did according to the word of*

Elijah, and she and he and her household ate for many days. The bowl of flour was not exhausted nor did the jar of oil become empty, according to the word of the LORD which He spoke through Elijah."

'Many days' here does not mean just several days but a long period of time. The flour and oil never running out is a work of creation. Then, how could Elijah manifest such a work of creation, which can be manifested only in the space of God?

Elijah did not possess the space of God, but at least for that moment, he read and received the heart and will of God limitatively. 'Limitatively' here means he read the heart of God about a certain thing for a certain moment in time. Sometimes God lets men read His heart to fulfill His will.

Elisha received the double portion of his master Elijah's inspiration, but when God did not let him understand, he did not even know why the Shunammite woman was troubled in heart. She gave birth to a son because she served the man of God Elisha with all her efforts. But her son suddenly died and when he did, she just went immediately to Elisha. But until she told him what happened, he could not know what her trouble was. *"When she came to the man of God to the hill, she caught hold of his feet. And Gehazi came near to push her away; but the man of God said, 'Let her alone, for her soul is troubled within her; and the LORD has hidden it from me and has not told me'"* (2 Kings 4:27).

In order to read God's heart and utilize His space, it is crucial to cultivate the heart of whole spirit so that we will trust God and obey Him completely. The reason why prophets like Elijah, Abraham, Moses, and Paul utilized the space of God was because they had the heart of whole spirit. When God commanded them to do something, they understood God's intention embedded in that command. They felt how God would work and they could picture it in their mind, and so they had spiritual confidence.

Elijah boldly proclaimed the living God and brought down fire from heaven because he felt in his heart what God would do. It was the same when he asked the widow of Zarephath to give him her last bit of food. If we have complete trust in God, we can obey even the things that do not make sense at all, and when we do that, it will be done as God has spoken. The work of creation took place for the widow because both the widow and Elijah fulfilled the measure of justice of God.

The widow trusted the man of God, Elijah, and she believed his word as God's Word itself. She obeyed his word without hesitation and without utilizing human thoughts. This way, she could participate in the space of God that Elijah was utilizing.

2 Chronicles 20:20 reads:

Put your trust in the LORD your God and you will be established. Put your trust in His prophets and succeed.

Elijah utilized God's space, which belongs to God exclusively, by trusting Him completely. The widow trusted this Elijah completely, and consequently the space of God came down upon them, and they saw the work of creation. As in the above case, God covers people with the space of God, if with faith and obedience they become united with men of God who utilize the space of God.

Daniel's Three Friends Unharmed in Furnace

Three friends of Daniel were thrown into a furnace only because they did not bow down to an idol. The furnace was seven times hotter than usual, and the soldiers who went near the furnace to throw them in were burned to death. Obviously those three men should have been burned to death, too. But what actually happened?

Daniel 3:24-25 says, *"Then Nebuchadnezzar the king was astounded and stood up in haste; he said to his high officials, 'Was it not three men we cast bound into the midst of the fire?' They replied to the king, 'Certainly, O king.' He said, 'Look! I see four men loosed and walking about in the midst of the fire without harm, and the appearance of the fourth is like a son of the gods!'"*

Certainly there were three men who were thrown into the furnace, but there were four men there. The king thought one of them was like a son of the gods. Basically people cannot see spiritual beings, but God opened the king's spiritual eyes and enabled him to see the spiritual being there. After the three men came out of the furnace, the people saw in regard to these men that the fire had no effect on the bodies of these men nor was the hair of their head singed, nor were their trousers damaged, nor had the smell of fire even come upon them (Daniel 3:27).

How could such a thing happen? The reason why Daniel's three friends were protected is because the space of God covered them. We can infer this from the phrase that a man 'like a son of gods' was with them. Of course, it is not 'gods' but the only God, but Nebuchadnezzar said so for he was a believer of gentile gods.

Then, who was this 'son of gods'? It was God the Holy Spirit. God the Holy Spirit Himself came down to them and God's space covered that physical space.

Moses changed bitter water of Marah into sweet water

Exodus chapter 15 depicts a scene where the bitter water of Marah turned into sweet water, and this is also an event done in the space of God. The sons of Israel crossed the Red Sea and came into the wilderness, and they could not get any water for three days. They found water at Marah, but it was bitter and not drinkable. Now they complained against Moses. When Moses prayed about it, God showed him a tree. When he threw it into the waters, the water turned sweet. Is it that the tree had some elements that could change the taste of water? No. God covered that water with the space of God and manifested a work of creation considering the faith and obedience of Moses.

The same kind of work of creation was manifested in our

church too and gave glory to God greatly. I prayed in Seoul that the salty water in Muan would change into sweet water, and the prayer was answered.

The water was from a well in Muan Manmin Church. It is located in Heje Myeon, Muan Goon, Jeonnam Province. It is completely surrounded by the sea, and when they dug a well, they could only get salty sea water. They installed a pipeline from a place 3km away to get fresh water, but they were still short of drinking water. The members of Muan Manmin Church remembered the sign manifested in Marah and believed the same thing could happen to them, and they prayed for it to happen. They asked me many times to come to Muan and pray for the salty water to be turned into sweet water.

In February 2000, I was doing a ten-day mountain prayer session, and I especially prayed for Muan Manmin Church. During that time the members of Muan Manmin Church also conducted relay-fasting to pray for the church and me, and they witnessed circular rainbows above their church every day for ten days.

After I finished my mountain prayer, I was inspired by the Holy Spirit to pray for the salty water in Muan to turn sweet. I did not go to Muan to pray for the wells there in person, but God worked transcending time and space to change the salty water into sweet water.

My prayer and the faith of the members of Muan Manmin Church fulfilled the justice of God and made this work of creation possible. Still today the well at Muan Manmin Church is springing up with sweet water. It's because it is covered by the space of God the Creator. Muan's sweet water was tested by FDA of the USA and proven to be healthy water that is rich in minerals. There are also so many healing works taking place through the water that the procession of pilgrims to the church never ceases.

The Dead Are Revived

The space of God can not only show work of creation but also it can control life and death. It can revive the dead or kill the living. It is for anything that has life— either plants or animals.

Numbers chapter 17 writes about the rod of Aaron that budded. It was possible because it was covered by the space of God. The dry rod put forth buds and produced blossoms, and it bore ripe almonds within a day's time. Even for a living tree, it would have taken months to do so, but it took place in a day, and it was a dry rod that produced fruit. It was possible because the rod was covered by the space of God.

When Jesus cursed the fig tree, it died soon, and it was also because the tree was covered by the space of God. *"...seeing a lone fig tree by the road, he came to it and found nothing on it except leaves only; and he said to it, 'no longer shall there ever be any fruit from you.' And at once the fig tree withered. Seeing this, the disciples were amazed and asked, 'How did the fig tree wither all at once?'"* (Matthew 21:19-20)

It was the case with Jesus reviving the dead Lazarus, too. In John chapter 11, we read Lazarus had been dead for four days and the body had foul smell. But when Jesus called him out, his spirit came back to him, and his decaying body was regenerated. Even the impossible in the physical space can be made possible in an instant in the space of God.

There was a teenage boy in our church who completely lost the sight in one of his eyes, but his vision was restored. He had cataract surgery on his left eye when he was three, but as a side-effect he had severe uveitis and detachment of the retina. His retina came off the ocular wall and he could not see well. To make it worse, he also had phthisis bulbi, or shrinking eyeball. Eventually he lost his sight of the left eye completely in 2006.

But in July 2007, he regained his sight through prayer. His left eye could not even sense any light, but he came to have 0.1 vision. His shrunken eyeball also recovered normal size. Furthermore, his right eye used to have 0.1 vision but it improved to 0.9. This case was presented along with detailed medical documents to more than 220 medical doctors from 41 countries in the 5th International Christian Medical Conference held in Norway under the auspices of WCDN (World Christian Doctors Network), and it was selected as the most impressive case among several other cases presented in the conference.

The same principle applies to all other organs, tissues, or nerves. Even if the nerves or the cells and tissues are dead due to accidents or diseases, they can become normal if they are covered by the space of God. Even the disabilities can be recovered in the space of God. Moreover, diseases that are caused by germs or viruses such as cancers, AIDS, tuberculosis, cold, or fever, can be cured in the space of God.

In the cases of diseases, the fire of the Holy Spirit comes and burns the germs or viruses first. Then, the part of the body that is damaged due to the disease recovers. Even for infertile couples, if the part of the body that had problem is covered by the space of God and recovers, they can succeed in conception. But to be healed of diseases and infirmities in the space of God, each one has to meet the qualifications of God's justice.

The Works that Transcend Time and Space

The works of power manifested in the space of God can be done transcending the limitations of time and space. It is possible because the space of God subdues and transcends other dimensions. Psalm 19:4 says, *"Their line has gone out through all the earth, and their utterances to the end of the world. In them He has placed a tent for the sun."* This means the Word of God spoken from the fourth heaven goes through to the end of the world.

Even a great distance in the first heaven, the physical space, is virtually the same as no distance in the space of God. Light travels around the Earth seven and a half times in a second. But the light of God's power can reach not just the end of the Earth but also the end of the universe within a blink of an eye. The physical distance has no meaning in the space of God.

In Matthew chapter 8, a centurion came to Jesus and asked Him to heal the sickness of one of his servants. Jesus said He would go with him, but he said, *"Lord, I am not worthy for You to come under my roof, but just say the word, and my servant will be healed"* (v. 8). So, Jesus replied to him, *"Go; it shall be done for you as you have believed"* (v. 13). At the very moment the servant was healed.

A sick person was healed being at another location when Jesus just commanded with His Words, because He possessed the space of God. The centurion could receive such a blessing because he showed complete faith in Jesus. Jesus also commended his faith saying, *"Truly I say to you, I have not found such great faith with anyone in Israel"* (v. 10).

To those children who are united with Him in faith God always shows the works of His power transcending time and space. Cynthia in Pakistan was dying of intestinal obstruction and Celiac disease. Cynthia's sister was in Korea at that time, and she brought Cynthia's photo to me to receive my prayer on the photo. The healing took place beyond the limitations of time and space. In the United States, Robert Johnson also received healing transcending time and space. He ruptured his Achilles tendon in a fall. He could not walk due to severe pain. He was told that surgery was necessary for it to heal, but wearing only a cast, he recovered completely without the surgical procedure in only nine weeks through prayer offered for him in Korea. This was a work of God's power manifested in the space of God.

Extraordinary Works of the Apostle Paul

In Acts chapter 19, it says God was performing extraordinary miracles by the hands of Paul. When he commanded in the name of Jesus Christ, evil spirits left and healing works took place even with handkerchiefs or aprons that had touched him. He was not harmed by the bite of a poisonous snake, and he also prophesied.

"God was performing extraordinary miracles by the hands of Paul, so that handkerchiefs or aprons were even carried from his body to the sick, and the diseases left them and the evil spirits went out" (Acts 19:11-12).

Likewise, God's powerful works can take place even through objects like handkerchiefs in the space of God. How extraordinary! There are many healing works taking place through the handkerchiefs on which I pray, too. The power of God never disappears or becomes extinct regardless of the passage of time as long as God's justice is not violated. Therefore, the handkerchiefs that contain the power of God are something very precious for it can open the space of God regardless of time and location.

But if they are used in an ungodly manner by a person who has no faith, no work of God will be manifested. Not just the one who is praying with the handkerchief but also the one who is prayed on must meet the qualifications of God's justice. They have to believe that the power of God is actually contained in it. The faith of the one who is praying for the sick person and the faith of the sick person will be accurately measured, and the work of God will be manifested as much as they are in accordance

151

with the justice of God.

Joshua Stopped the Sun and the Moon

The reason why higher dimensions can subdue lower dimensions is that the strength of light and the flow of time are different. The higher dimension of space, the brighter the light and faster the flow of time. The light of the fourth heaven is the brightest and then the third, and second heaven.

In regard to the flow of time, it is faster in the second heaven than the first heaven, and it is even faster in the third heaven. But in the fourth heaven, it can be either faster or slower. It will be operated as God harbors in His heart. God can extend it, shorten it, or even stop it.

The works of creation, the dead coming back to life, and divine healing taking place transcending time and space, are all made possible with the time flow that came to a halt. That's why the particular event can take place as soon as it is harbored in heart or as soon as the command is given.

When Joshua had a battle with the Amorites, the sun and the moon stood still, and it was 'extension of flow of time'. Joshua 10:13 says, *"So the sun stood still, and the moon stopped, until the nation avenged themselves of their enemies."* This was when Joshua had a battle against the Amorites during the conquest of the Canaan Land. What are the factors that can cause the sun to stand still all day in the first heaven?

The Earth has to rotate itself once a day, and for the sun to stop, the Earth has to stop rotating. If the Earth stops rotating even for a moment, the impact will be huge not just for Earth itself but also for many other celestial bodies. But how could the sun stop all day?

We can find the answer in the space of God. At that moment, God covered not just Earth but also the whole first heaven with the space of God. Thus, at least for that moment, everything in the first heaven was synchronized with the flow of time in spiritual realm. It was the extended flow of time. The sun stood still for the whole day, so people might have felt a long time had passed. But in fact, it could have been just one minute, or even one second.

At that time, the whole first heaven was on the flow of time of the spiritual realm, so physical flow of time was not in effect at all. Even if just a particular part of the first heaven and not the whole first heaven was covered by the space of God, there wouldn't be any problem, because other parts of the physical space would still be under the flow of time of the physical space.

Elijah ran faster than the chariot of the king

In the Bible, we can see a case in which somebody was in the shortened time flow. It was when Elijah ran ahead of the chariot of King Ahab, which is recorded in 1 Kings 18. The shortened time flow is the opposite of extended time flow. Suppose one is covered by the space of the fourth dimension for one hour in physical time. In the space of God, he can shorten this one hour as he wants. If he shortens it to 30 minutes, it doesn't mean the other 30 minutes disappeared. It means one hour is compressed into 30 minutes.

For example, suppose you put a 100 meter-long cloth, and ran from one end to the other end, and it took 20 seconds. Then, if you fold the cloth into a half, how long would it take? It is 50 meters, so it will take about 10 seconds. If you fold the cloth again, the length is shortened, and the time is contracted. But the cloth didn't disappear.

It is somewhat similar with shortening the time in the space of God. Elijah ran at his own speed, but he could run faster than the chariot of the king because he was in the shortened time-flow. Usually, commercial airplanes fly at the speed of around 900km, but the passengers in the plane do not feel the speed.

1 Kings 18:46 reads, *"Then the hand of the LORD was on Elijah, and he girded up his loins and outran Ahab to Jezreel."* King Ahab was hurrying in his chariot to avoid rain, and Elijah ran faster than this chariot. He could run faster than a chariot because he used the space of God which has no limitations of time and space. The Bible says that 'the hand of the LORD was on Elijah'. By the power of God, Elijah's body was covered by His power and something beyond human limitations took place.

Moving through Spiritual Space

In Acts chapter 8, Philip received the guidance of the Holy

Spirit to meet the Ethiopian eunuch on the way to Jerusalem. He preached the gospel of Jesus Christ to this eunuch and even baptized him. Philip was in the desert on the road to Gaza but in a moment he appeared in Azotus. It was actually movement through spiritual space similar to 'teleportation.' *"When they came up out of the water, the Spirit of the Lord snatched Philip away; and the eunuch no longer saw him, but went on his way rejoicing. But Philip found himself at Azotus, and as he passed through he kept preaching the gospel to all the cities until he came to Caesarea"* (Acts 8:39-40).

For a teleportation to take place, one has to go through the spiritual passageway that is formed by the space of God. As the time flow comes to a stop in that spiritual passage, one can be teleported.

God let our church members indirectly experience this kind of moving in the spiritual space. It was through the dragonflies. Dragonflies that were in other areas came to where we were and disappeared through the spiritual passageway formed by the space of God.

Swarms of dragonflies appeared where we were conducting our summer retreat, and they ate up mosquitoes and other harmful insects. At that time, mature dragonflies moved from one place to another. It was 2006 when the moving of the dragonflies in this way first began. This can be categorized into horizontal movement and vertical movement, according to the kind of spiritual passageway.

What is more amazing is that when the church members

called the dragonflies, they weren't afraid of the people but sat on the finger tips and other parts of the body of the church members. Dragonflies are beneficial because they eat harmful insects in summer. I recall that in my childhood it was very difficult to catch a single dragonfly. They would fly off if they sensed the slightest bit of human presence nearby. For some time now it has been very difficult to see a single dragonfly in Seoul, and the appearance of swarms of dragonflies is certainly a work of God.

The following year, 2007, the dragonflies began to appear beginning in early July. Dragonflies usually appear from late summer through autumn. While the dragonflies that were still larvae were passing through the spiritual passageway, those larvae matured to become adults. As they were passing through the fourth dimensional space, their growth was accelerated. So, the dragonflies could appear much earlier in that year than usual.

Moreover, in 2008, not only the time of their appearing but also the number of the dragonflies was controlled. Endless swarms of dragonflies began to pour down from the sky starting in the first week of July. Different mission groups of our church had their respective summer retreats in different locations of South Korea, and all the church members witnessed the dragonflies coming down vertically from around the sun. The dragonflies did not go to other places locally. They came down and stayed in the areas where they descended and they could be seen sitting on the hands, faces, or shoulders of the church members.

The theme of the summer retreat that year was 'Spiritual

Space', and the joy of the believers was just great. They could understand the message having a real life example of the dragonflies moving through the spiritual space and coming to them. Through this retreat the faith of the church members increased to a higher step. The same kind of work took place for all the branch churches not only in Korea but all over the world.

The same kind of event took place in the summer of 2009, too. Each mission group had their summer retreat respectively, and there were more dragonflies that appeared than the years before. The believers saw tens of thousands of dragonflies coming down from around the sun, through the spiritual space that was opened. As they were coming down from the sky they sparkled and looked like flakes of snow.

When the sons of Israel were crossing the Red Sea that was parted by strong winds, a spiritual passageway was formed there for them. How strong the winds must have been to have been able to part the sea! A man wouldn't be able to stand up there in such winds. But more than two million Israelites peacefully walked the midst of the winds. This is because a spiritual passageway was formed to block the winds from affecting the people. Then, what happened when they were crossing the Jordan River to go into the Canaan Land?

Joshua 3:15-16 says, *"...and when those who carried the ark came into the Jordan, and the feet of the priests carrying the ark were dipped in the edge of the water (for the Jordan overflows all its banks all the days of harvest), the waters*

*which were flowing down from above stood and rose up in one
heap, a great distance away at Adam, the city that is beside
Zarethan; and those which were flowing down toward the sea
of the Arabah, the Salt Sea, were completely cut off. So the
people crossed opposite Jericho."*

From the point where the sons of Israel were, the waters
upstream were piled up in one heap and the downstream just
kept on flowing. At this time, a spiritual space was made in a
shape to similar something like a dam.

Various Ways in which Spiritual Passageways Have Been Utilized

If we can utilize this spiritual passage very well, we can also
control the weather conditions. For example, suppose two
specific areas are suffering, one from flooding and the other from
drought. Then, if we move the rain clouds from the flooding area
to the dry area, then, we can resolve the problem of both areas.

The unexpected rainfall in Israel is such an example. In
September 2009, I prayed for a certain thing while I was
preparing for a crusade in Israel. Israel was having a hard time due
to severe drought that had persisted for the past five years. The
pastors in Israel explained their situation and asked me to pray
about it.

If such a request, which is at a national level of interest, is
to be answered, there are some conditions that have to be met.
This is that the president or equivalent level leaders must ask for

the prayer with faith, or a majority of the people should make a request for the prayer with faith. But feeling very sorry for their situation I just prayed on the first and second day of the crusade for a rainfall in Israel to quench their drought.

What was the result? Israel has a clear distinction between the rainy reason and dry season. September is dry season, and it rarely rains in September. Sometimes it may begin to rain a little bit beginning in late October, and the actual rainy season is from December through February of the coming year. Also, due to the long drought, the level of the Sea of Galilee was reaching the lower red line, which is 208 meters. This is the lower limit at which water could no longer be drawn from the Sea.

But one day after the crusade was over, the northern part of Israel had rain. On September 13, a Sunday, they had a significant amount of rainfall in Jerusalem and also Tel Aviv. The Israeli pastors rejoiced and gave glory to God saying they had rain thanks to my prayer. But it was not finished. They had more rainfall the next week, and the Israeli Water Resources Department said the amount of rainfall for just two days was the same as the sum of the average rainfall for both September and October. It was not something possible according to the justice of God, but God heard the prayer and going beyond justice He allowed for them to have rain.

There are also so many typhoons and hurricanes that bring about calamities around the world. If we can move the courses of typhoons or hurricanes to uninhabited areas, there won't be any problem.

Two typhoons were approaching the Philippines when I went there for the crusade in 2001. The 16th typhoon "Nari" and the 19th typhoon "Lekima" were approaching the Philippines with strong hurricane force winds. If the typhoons had come according to the forecasted paths, we wouldn't have been able to have the crusade. At the press conference there, the reporters asked me whether the crusade would be possible because of the typhoons.

At that time I said, "The typhoons will die out or change their directions. There won't be any typhoon or rain during the crusade, so please, try to attend it." The Nari died out just before the crusade, and the Lekima suddenly changed its course, by-passing the Philippines. We were able to have the crusade without any problems.

We can stop not only typhoons but also other natural disasters such as volcanic eruptions or earthquakes if we utilize the spiritual space. We can just cover the source of volcano eruption or the earthquake with the space of God, and these things can be made possible when it is right according to the justice of God. For example, to stop a disaster that causes damage at a national level, the leader of the country is supposed to ask for the prayer. Also, even if the spiritual space is open, the justice of the first heaven cannot be totally ignored. The working of the spiritual space will be limited to the extent where there will be no confusion in the first heaven after the spiritual space is lifted.

God governs all the heavens with His omnipotence, and He is the God of love and justice.

Love that Transcends Justice

In Genesis chapter 18, we can read that God foretold Abraham what would happen to the corrupted Sodom and Gomorrah. *"And the LORD said, 'The outcry of Sodom and Gomorrah is indeed great, and their sin is exceedingly grave. I will go down now, and see if they have done entirely according to its outcry, which has come to Me; and if not, I will know'"* (Genesis 18:20-21).

Sodom and Gomorrah had to be punished for their sins according to the rules of justice, but God let Abraham know about it in advance because his nephew Lot was living there. It was the heart of God who wanted to give them another chance. This is the love and justice of God.

Then, Abraham asked God five times to save Sodom. At first, he asked not to destroy it if there were fifty righteous men, and then forty five, then forty, thirty, twenty, and finally the number went down to just ten. *"Then he said, 'Oh may the LORD not be angry, and I shall speak only this once; suppose ten are found there?' And He said, 'I will not destroy it on account of the ten'"* (Genesis 18:32).

As a mere creature Abraham could ask God so boldly. This shows us he had the heart of the Lord and became one with God. He asked with earnest love to move the heart of God and save the people, and God was touched by his love and promised to do what he asked.

God works with love within the boundary of justice. So, He wanted to show mercy and compassion even when He was punishing Sodom and Gomorrah, and He did give another opportunity with love that transcended justice through the prayer of the righteous man Abraham.

Sodom and Gomorrah were eventually punished for they did not even have ten righteous men among them, but Abraham's nephew Lot and his family were saved. It was because Lot was in the space of Abraham, who was very much loved by God. In other words, because God loved Abraham so much, God covered Lot and his family with spiritual space thinking of Abraham.

As explained, everything can be controlled in the love and justice of God in the space of God. Love annuls justice without violating it. To make such things happen, one has to cultivate the heart that is in accordance with the justice of the fourth heaven. Namely, when one has cultivated the heart that is one with God's heart, he can show the works of God that go beyond justice without violating the justice of the fourth heaven.

The problem is how one can cultivate the heart of God. Until this is done, with only faith and love one has to overcome tremendous trials that are unimaginable for men. He has to pay the price in accordance with the justice of God, by going through each step in trials, until he is enabled to utilize the space of God having learned the justice of the fourth heaven.

Abraham also had many trials and tests until he was called 'a friend of God'. When he turned seventy five years old God told him that a great nation would be formed through him, but for more than twenty years he did not beget a child. But when he was ninety nine years old, when Sarah was eighty nine and could not conceive a child, God finally told him that he would get a son the following year.

This was completely impossible by human knowledge, but Abraham put his trust in God and never doubted. God recognized his faith as righteousness, and as he believed he begot Isaac. But when Isaac was growing up and so lovely, God told Abraham to sacrifice Isaac as a burnt offering. Abraham believed that God would revive him even if he gave Isaac as a burnt offering, for God had already told him that many descendants would come forth through Isaac. He was able to give his only son, Isaac, without any hesitation because he truly revered God.

After Abraham passed all the trials and tests, God called him 'a friend of God' and established him as the 'father of faith'. After the final test of giving his only son Isaac as a burnt offering, he received all the blessings that a man can receive, such as blessings of children, health, wealth, and long life.

God is looking for true children who can receive blessings and lead numerous souls to the way of salvation through prayer of faith and love like Abraham did. God shows us works of creation, controlling the life and death, and works that transcend space and time because He wants true children who have the heart of God.

Genesis 18:17-19 says, *"The LORD said, 'Shall I hide from Abraham what I am about to do, since Abraham will surely become a great and mighty nation, and in him all the nations of the earth will be blessed? 'For I have chosen him, so that he may command his children and his household after him to keep the way of the LORD by doing righteousness and justice, so that the LORD may bring upon Abraham what He has spoken about him.'"*

If only we can understand the basic principles of God's space that are explained up until this point, we can understand many events in the Bible in more depth, and we can also experience them in our lives, too. We can go beyond human limitations if we become God's true children by believing in God and recovering His lost image. For this reason the resurrected Lord Jesus gave us the last word before He ascended into Heaven. *"...but you will receive power when the Holy Spirit has come upon you; and you shall be My witnesses both in Jerusalem, and in all Judea and Samaria, and even to the remotest part of the earth"* (Acts 1:8).

What is the shortcut to receiving the power of God and becoming the witness of the Lord? It is to sanctify our heart, and to pray fervently to become a person of whole spirit, so that we will be able to utilize the space of God. Furthermore, we should strive to cultivate God's justice and love completely to be able to inherit the most beautiful heavenly dwelling place New Jerusalem and even the space of God.

Chapter 2
God's Image

One can recover the lost image of God once he becomes a true child of God
who has the heart of God. But it does not mean he can become like God Himself.
God can exist as just light without any form, or He might put on a certain form.

God Put On a Form for Human Cultivation

Man Is Created After the Image of God

We Can't See God's Face Directly

Size of God's Form

God's Image in Apostle John's View

Partake in Divine Nature

What kind of appearance does God have? How big might He be?

As one has accepted Jesus Christ and comes to know more about God, he should become curious about the image of God as well as the kingdom of heaven. When children are separated from their parents for a long time they would miss their parents and cherish them. It is similar to us seeking God and yearning for Him deep in our nature.

Matthew 5:8 says, *"Blessed are the pure in heart, for they shall see God."* 'To be pure in heart' means 'not setting one's mind on meaningless things but to be pure and clean in the truth.' It is a heart that is blameless and spotless and with which we do not think anything evil or of rudeness. It says the pure in heart will see God, and what does this mean? It does not mean they will see God's original entity itself. It means that they will experience God by receiving anything they ask God.

But it does not mean men can never see God's image at all. It just means they cannot see God's face directly (Exodus 33:20). God is spirit, so we cannot know the image of God completely because we are not able to see God directly. But God says we are

167

created in His image, so we can just infer that God and we share something in common in our appearance. We can imagine what God might look like from the Bible, which is a revelation about God.

God Put On a Form for Human Cultivation

We find in Exodus 3:14 God explains Himself as *"I AM WHO I AM."* He is the perfect being who exists by Himself from before eternity. Men have limited knowledge, so we think there must be a beginning to everything. That is why God uses the word 'beginning' but it is only for our understanding.

John 1:1 reads, *"In the beginning was the Word, and the Word was with God, and the Word was God."* And Genesis 1:1 says, *"In the beginning God created the heavens and the earth."*

God created men when He was creating the heavens and the earth and all things in them, and thus, the 'beginning' in the book of Genesis establishes a relation with men. On the other hand, the beginning mentioned in John chapter 1 is a point in time that was way before the time of creation. Furthermore, it has no relation to men.

In the beginning God existed in a space that is a spiritual realm, which is invisible to our eyes. God existed as a beautiful and brilliant light and ruled over everything hovering over all the spaces of the universe. God had humanity as well as divinity, and for this reason He planned human cultivation to gain true children and began to exist as the Trinity: the Father, the Son, and the Holy Spirit.

It was at that moment that God began to have an image. Genesis 1:26 says, *"Then God said, 'Let Us make man in Our image, according to Our likeness...'"*

Of course, it is not a physical form like that of men. It was a spiritual image to embody God who is spirit. Angels, the heavenly army, or cherubim are all spiritual beings but they do have respective forms. God in the beginning did not have a specific form, but at some point He came to have a specific form.

God the Trinity put on a form for us men, and when God created the Earth, which is the stage for human cultivation, He came down to this Earth. He searched for what the Earth would need in the future and how He would make those things. Then He began the actual creation of all things.

Man is Created after the Image of God

God the Trinity created men in His image on the sixth day of the Creation. This does not mean that only outward appearance of man was after the image of God. It also means our heart was created after the heart of God.

But since the disobedience of Adam, men lost the original image that they received when they were created, and they were increasingly stained with sins. Adam losing the image of God does not mean the outward image disappeared, but it means he lost the nature of God, which is a holy fragrance. Men are composed of spirit, soul, and body, but as a result of sin, the spirit of all men 'died.' From that time on, they became no different from animals that were created with only soul and body.

But when the time came, God sent Jesus to this earth to open the way of salvation so that everyone could be saved. To anyone who accepts Jesus Christ, God gives him the Holy Spirit as a gift. Then, his dead spirit will be revived, and he can begin to recover the lost image of God. The holy God wants His children to have holiness in them, as well. That is why He urgingly advises us saying, *"You shall be holy, for I am holy"* (1 Peter 1:16).

God does not look at the appearance but the heart of each person. We can become God's true children if we struggle against and throw away sins to the point of shedding blood and cast off all forms of evil. We can recover the lost image of God and give out strong lights from our spiritual form to the extent that we resemble God who is Light.

1 John 5:18 says, *"We know that no one who is born of God sins; but He who was born of God keeps him, and the evil one does not touch him."* God protects those who live by the Word of God and do not sin. Because of their bright light, the enemy devil and Satan cannot even come near them.

The purpose of God creating the world and men is to gain true children who have the image of God. But almost every man since the time of creation has not cultivated or did not cultivate the image of God. There have been countless people born since Adam, but only a handful of them actually cultivated the kind of heart that God wanted them to have. Such people walked with God and revealed His glory in their lives. They performed powerful works that were beyond human imagination. Elijah brought down fire from Heaven; Abraham virtually offered his only son Isaac as a sacrifice; the apostle Paul was faithful with all his life and love. When God saw people such as these, He was so joyous.

On the contrary, even among those who were used for the kingdom of God, there were some people who could not really be considered as 'true men of God.' For example, in case of Elisha, he learned everything from Elijah and received a double portion of Elijah's inspiration. But his heart was not as perfect as that of Elijah (2 Kings 2:24). When children followed and mocked him intolerably, he eventually cursed them. Two female bears came out and ripped up forty-two children.

Lot also saw the goodness of Abraham, and yet he could not cultivate Abraham's heart of goodness. He received material blessings thanks to Abraham and in a dangerous situation his life was saved by Abraham. Still, he could not cultivate a perfect heart.

Elisha performed many amazing things and people said he was a man of God. But it was just that people respected him as a prophet. A true man of God is not just a person who can be used by God to serve God's purpose for the moment. It is a person who has recovered the image of God having a holy and pure heart that is free of any blemish or spot.

We Can't See God's Face Directly

Since the fall of Adam, nobody in the first heaven has been able to directly see the face of God who is Light itself. God is spirit and we cannot see Him with physical eyes. Moreover, Exodus 33:20 says, *"You cannot see My face, for no man can see Me and live!"*

Elijah was caught up to Heaven without seeing death, and yet he could not look at God directly. 1 Kings 19:12-13 says, *"After the earthquake a fire, but the LORD was not in the fire; and after the fire a sound of a gentle blowing. When Elijah heard it, he wrapped his face in his mantle and went out and stood in the entrance of the cave. And behold, a voice came to him and said, 'What are you doing here, Elijah?'"* Elijah had wrapped his face in his mantle just at hearing a slight sound from God.

Judges 13:22 also says, *"So Manoah said to his wife, 'We will surely die, for we have seen God.'"* Manoah is the father of Samson. Isaiah also said, *"Woe is me, for I am ruined! Because I am a man of unclean lips, and I live among a people of unclean lips; for my eyes have seen the King, the LORD of hosts"* (Isaiah 6:5).

People were killed even when they violated a place or object that was set apart for God. It was the case with the men at Bethshemesh who were put to death because they had looked into the ark of the LORD (1 Samuel 6:19).

Because men die if they see the face of God directly, God has revealed Himself indirectly. He showed Himself in the flame on the bush, or in the fire or in clouds. Sometimes He showed Himself in wonders such as parting the Red Sea and stopping the sun and the moon; or in signs such as the lame standing up, the blind coming to see, the deaf coming to hear, the mute coming to speak, or the dead being revived.

God also showed His image through the Lord Jesus as said in Colossians 1:15 *"He is the image of the invisible God, the firstborn of all creation."* John 1:18 says, *"No one has seen God at any time; the only begotten God who is in the bosom of the Father, He has explained Him"* and in John 14:9 Jesus says *"He who has seen Me has seen the Father; how can you say, 'Show us the Father'?"*

Today, many people say they believe in God but they don't truly know who He is, and they don't understand His heart and will. They imagine what God is like within their own self-conceptualizations. It is like a frog living in a well thinks the small, round sky it is seeing is the whole sky. Likewise, those people cannot share true love with God the Father, and moreover, when they see those who are loved by God, they think it is strange.

Jesus Showed the Image of God

Why does Jesus say in John 14:9, *"He who has seen Me has seen the Father"?* Jesus is in the Father God, and God is in Jesus, and thus They are completely one. For this reason, the words Jesus spoke were not of His own but given by the Father God.

In John 12:49-50, He said, *"For I did not speak on My own initiative, but the Father Himself who sent Me has given Me a commandment as to what to say and what to speak. 'I know that His commandment is eternal life; therefore the things I speak, I speak just as the Father has told Me'"* and in Matthew 15:30-31, *"And large crowds came to Him, bringing with them those who were lame, crippled, blind, mute, and many others, and they laid them down at His feet; and He healed them. So the crowd marveled as they saw the mute speaking, the crippled restored, and the lame walking, and the blind seeing; and they glorified the God of Israel."*

When Jesus testified to the Father with words, God showed that He is almighty through signs, wonders, and extraordinary and wondrous things. Those who believed and followed Jesus could see the power of God and gave glory to God. But those who did not believe Jesus left Him and scattered. They did not believe Jesus even though they witnessed amazing works of God, just because those things did not agree with their own theories and knowledge.

Jesus voluntarily took the wretched way of cross to fulfill the Jesus voluntarily took the wretched way of cross to fulfill the providence of salvation because He was completely one with God the Father. He had one heart with God who wanted to save mankind, the sinners, even though the way was the way of suffering. He had the same will with God in that He Himself had to become the atoning sacrifice. For this reason Jesus took the way without any reluctance although it was such a narrow and difficult way to take in men's way of thinking.

Why mustn't we make an image of God?

In Exodus chapter 3, God called Moses from the flame of fire in the bush at Mount Horeb. He told him to lead the sons of Israel who were suffering in Egypt to the promised land of Canaan. What is the reason that God appeared in the flame on the bush?

Obviously when bushes catch fire they will be consumed. It was something out of the ordinary that the bushes were not consumed by the fire nor did the flame disappear. God intended to let Moses see that there is a spiritual, imperishable world.

Also, a bush has been considered to symbolize a 'curse' and thus, God's messenger appearing in the flame of fire in the bushes means that God is the one who controls even the cursed bush. This in turn represents in spiritual sense that the enemy devil and Satan are under the control of God. Moses became a person who was qualified in the sight of God through forty years of trial, and finally God called him to make him the leader of Israel.

But later, when God revealed Himself to the sons of Israel in the flames at Mount Horeb, they only heard His voice but did not see any image. Again, God reminded them of this fact later and strongly forbade them to make any image. *"So watch yourselves carefully, since you did not see any form on the day the LORD spoke to you at Horeb from the midst of the fire, so that you do not act corruptly and make a graven image for yourselves in the form of any figure, the likeness of male or female, the likeness of any animal that is on the earth, the likeness of any winged bird that flies in the sky, the likeness of anything that creeps on the ground, the likeness of any fish that is in the water below the earth. And beware not to lift up your eyes to heaven and see the sun and the moon and the stars, all the host of heaven, and be drawn away and worship them and serve them, those which the LORD your God has allotted to all the peoples under the whole heaven"* (Deuteronomy 4:15-19).

What is the reason God said this? Men were created with a fixed form, and thus they have a tendency to make the form of God, too. God was worried that if they did, they would limit the nature of God within the framework of a fixed image. If they made an image of God, it would not help them understand Him better, but it would rather disable them from seeing the true image of God by being deceived by the 'false' image. In turn, this might lead them to worship idols, which is one of the things that God hates the most.

God is spirit, and how can we make an image of Him and express Him? So, when Moses asked God to show Himself to him, He promised that He would show all the images of goodness rather than an actual, material image.

Just as water freezes to become ice, or boils to become vapor, God can show Himself in various forms having the one nature.

In this way He is helping men to understand Him better, for He is spirit and men have their physical limitations.

The Size of God's Form

Many parts of the Bible have some expressions about God's body parts such as, 'Your eyes' (1 Kings 8:29), 'ear' (Nehemiah 1:6), and 'hands' (Isaiah 65:2). Do these expressions have only symbolic meanings? That is not the case.

God does not exist as a formless void. He has a certain form which means He is clearly substance. But He is different from humans in a sense that He has a form that is of spirit itself without a physical body while men have spirit, soul, and body. God is in the form of brilliant lights, and we cannot see Him directly. Furthermore, He is fundamentally different from men in a sense that Adam first had a form and then was filled with the truth, while God is the truth itself and then He came to have a form.

Some may think God exists in a very big body for He is the Creator who created all things in the universe and rules over them. Of course, He has a big form, but He can change His form freely. Therefore, we cannot understand what His form is like if we think with human understanding.

Even after we enter into Heaven, we have a fundamental difference from God. Men will have the spiritual body which went through human cultivation in a physical body on this earth. However, God can either have a form or get out of the current form. But men will be confined to a certain form that will not be changed forever in Heaven. It is somewhat like we can make any form with plaster, but once we complete making a certain form we cannot return it to original substance.

God can exist as only light without having a form, or He can also put on a form. In the fourth heaven, God does not usually put on a form and He just exists as light and voice. But He puts on a form when He is with the prophets or when He comes down to the third heaven, the heavenly kingdom. He puts on a form when He is in a place where He should put the form on, and He does not have a form when He doesn't have to. He can even freely control the size of His form.

For example, in the fourth heaven a substance is not fixed as a solid, liquid, or gas. The same substance can change its form as freely as God harbors it in His heart. So, God originally existed as light and sound that did not have a form, but when He comes down to the third heaven He can have a specific form.

The first man, Adam, was made after this image, the image of God in the third heaven, which is also the image that we will see when we get to Heaven. But even if He has the same form, He appears differently between when He is in the fourth heaven and when He is in the third heaven. It is because the light, glory, dignity, and all things look different according to the different dimensions.

For example, even the same piece of crystal will look different according to kinds of lights and the setting where the crystal is placed. Likewise, the glory and shape of the original

God in the fourth heaven look different in a space that is of a lower dimension. Even in the same spiritual realm, the forms look different according to the different dimension, and the differences will be much more if God comes down to the first heaven, the physical space.

Moreover, seeing God from this physical world through an open passage to the spiritual realm and seeing God who has come down to this earth having put on a limited physical space, are completely different. The prophets or the angels cannot put on the limited physical space, so even if they appear in the physical space, they are still in the space of spirit. But God can put on any space as He harbors in His heart for He is the Creator who created all sorts of spaces. He can appear in the physical space being in the spiritual space, and He can also appear in a physical form, which is visible to men.

God appearing through spiritual passages

We can find many records in the Bible about God Himself coming down to this earth in the course of human cultivation. How did God come down to this earth?

As Genesis 11:5 reads, *"The LORD came down to see the city and the tower which the sons of men had built,"* God Himself came down to this earth to see what people were doing. And He descended to see Moses as written in Exodus 19:18, *"Now Mount Sinai was all in smoke because the LORD descended upon it in fire; and its smoke ascended like the*

smoke of a furnace, and the whole mountain quaked violently"
and in Numbers 11:25, *"Then the LORD came down in the
cloud and spoke to him; and He took of the Spirit who was
upon him and placed Him upon the seventy elders. And when
the Spirit rested upon them, they prophesied. But they did not
do it again."*

God is not bound by the changes in the flow of time. All the
physical and spiritual spaces belong to Him. But the fact remains
that He still used a spiritual passageway to come down to this
earth. He didn't have to come through the spiritual passage, but
He did so not to break the rules of justice Himself.

Even though God Himself was there, men of flesh at that time
could not see Him. But those whose spiritual eyes were opened
and who communicated with God could see God according to
the extent to which they had come into spirit. Of course, it is not
to see God face to face, but they could see and feel Him within
the limitations allowed by God.

Exodus 33:11 says, *"Thus the LORD used to speak to Moses
face to face, just as a man speaks to his friend."* But this does
not mean Moses saw the face of God directly. It means God
showed Himself to Moses in a special way that Moses would not
die even after seeing the glory of God. It was because Moses was
meeker and more humble than anybody else on the face of the
earth, and he was faithful in all God's house.

Exodus 33:18-19 says, *"Then Moses said, 'I pray You,
show me Your glory!' And He said, 'I Myself will make all
My goodness pass before you, and will proclaim the name of*

*the LORD before you; and I will be gracious to whom I will
be gracious, and will show compassion on whom I will show
compassion.'"*

But in Exodus 33:23, we can understand that Moses did not
see God's face but His back. He was more humble and meeker
than anyone else on the face of the earth and faithful in all God's
house, and yet he could not see God's image directly for he was
bound by the limitations of the physical body.

God appeared to Abraham

In Genesis chapter 18, we read that Abraham served three
persons with all his best. This was the occasion when God the
Holy Spirit and two archangels appeared in a human form. God
the Holy Spirit is one with God the Father, and He can appear in
a human form having put on the physical space as He harbors it
in His heart.

How, then, could the two archangels appear in a human
form? They cannot put on a physical space by their own ability,
but it was made possible because they were with God the Holy
Spirit in the space of God the Holy Spirit. But God the Holy
Spirit and the two archangels appearing in a human form does
not mean they were the same as human beings. It was just that
they put on a human form on top of their spiritual form so that
their spiritual form could be seen in the physical space.

The three of them, namely God the Holy Spirit and the two
archangels ate the food that Abraham served them (Genesis

18:8), but their eating was different from men's eating. They didn't chew and digest the food like men did, but as soon as they ate, the food just disappeared into air. It is much like the resurrected Lord ate some food and the food was kind of dissolved and eliminated through the breathing. Of course, having put on the physical space for a moment was not the same as being in a resurrected body. The resurrected body is a physical body on this earth that changed into a spiritual body, but for the three persons at that time, they momentarily existed in the body that was appropriate to be in the physical space as needed.

The reason why God the Holy Spirit had to come down to this earth with two archangels having put on a physical space was that He had to have a look at Sodom and Gomorrah directly. Of course, He could have come down in spirit to do that, but He had a reason to go to the land and see them in person.

The two archangels appeared in human form, and that is why they could certainly check how corrupted the people there were. They saw the beauty of the two archangels and sought to do evil to them. God the Holy Spirit and two archangels could directly experience and feel the evil of the people of Sodom and Gomorrah because they came in actual human form before them.

Genesis 18:13 says, *"And the LORD said to Abraham..."* From this we can infer that the one who appeared before Abraham was the LORD God. But it says he saw three persons so that we can understand the way God appeared in front of

Abraham.

There were several ways in which God appeared before Abraham. He could show Himself to Abraham in a dream or vision, or He could have just given him His voice. These were the methods that opened the spiritual space before Abraham who was in the physical space so that he could see and feel God who was in the spiritual space. In such cases, one can see God and hear His voice only when his spiritual eyes and ears are opened. If one's spiritual eyes are not opened, he can never see what is going on in spirit, even though God is with him.

But when God appeared along with two archangels, it was a completely different case. At that time, it was not just opening spiritual space in the physical space to make Himself visible in the physical space. It was a case where He actually came out to the physical space. Though to a limited degree, He put on a physical space and came out to the physical space.

If the former is like seeing God's image on TV, the latter is like God came out of the TV. If God comes out to the physical space having put on the limited physical space, people can see Him even though their spiritual eyes are not opened, and in such case God can be seen as a human being.

The Lord in the form of strong brilliance

Now, what does the appearance of God the Son look like? Sometimes we hear from people who say they saw the Lord in dreams or visions. Most of them say He was full of mercy and love, and it is because He took His light away to show Himself in an appearance full of mercy. If He shows the divine authority and dignity which is at the same level as God the Creator, nobody would dare to look at Him directly.

This is the reason why we cannot see the Lord in Heaven unless we pursue peace with all men, and sanctification (Hebrews 12:14). The light of the Lord is just too strong. Only those who go into spirit and whole spirit will be able to see the Lord because the light of their own spiritual body will also be strong.

The apostle John saw the appearance of the Lord in his vision. He described the eyes, feet, and hair of the Lord in detail. We can also imagine the appearance of God the Father from the description of the Lord's appearance.

Revelation 1:14-15 says, *"His head and His hair were white like white wool, like snow; and His eyes were like a flame of fire. His feet were like burnished bronze, when it has been made to glow in a furnace, and His voice was like the sound of many waters."*

It says the Lord's hair was white like white wool, and this means that He is free of evil, and He stands in the midst of the perfect goodness. It says His eyes are like a flame of fire, but it does not mean His eyes are fearful. It means they brighten the surroundings and make others feel warm. It also means they burn all the sins and evil. Nobody can hide from the eyes of the Lord, and everything will be clearly revealed before Him. It says His feet are like burnished bronze. The more you refine it, the purer the bronze will be. Many times in literature they compare the eyes of a beautiful woman with twinkling stars or the lips with cherries. Similarly John compared the Lord's feet with burnished bronze. Feet are the body parts that people consider the dirtiest. And John wrote that even the feet of the Lord are most holy and dignified.

Revelation 1:16-17 also says, *"...and His face was like the sun shining in its strength. When I saw Him, I fell at His feet like a dead man. And He placed His right hand on me, saying, 'Do not be afraid; I am the first and the last...'"*

The apostle John was a sanctified and proper man to receive revelations of God, but he became like a dead person before the Lord. The Lord placed His right hand on John telling him not to be afraid. It means the Lord gave him the duty to write the book of Revelation which will awaken the many at the end time by sealing him laying His hand. Also, it was that the Lord comforted John so he could fulfill his duty in peace.

God's Image in Apostle John's View

The apostle John saw the throne of God and things around it and wrote about them in Revelation chapter 4. He saw an event that would take place a very long time after he recorded it. As in this case, with God's permission, we can be at any place and any point in time whether past or future, transcending space and time. We can see Heaven and Hell, the time before the Creation, and also the Great White Throne Judgment that will take place in the future.

In the case of the apostle John, his spirit was separated to see the spiritual realm. Here, the separation of spirit refers to one's spirit coming out of his body. One can see the spiritual realm through a vision, too, but in a vision he can see only parts. For this reason when God wants to show us a broader picture, He works through the separation of spirit. Then, how could the apostle John see God and His throne?

He had undergone so many trials and persecutions in the name of the Lord until he turned ninety. He was thrown into a pot of boiling oil, but he did not die by the work of God. He eventually was exiled to the Patmos Island. He received revelations from God having deep prayers in the island. He by that time had been completely sanctified through deep prayers and many trials that he had gone through. He received revelations in the state of holiness, and that is why his spirit could go as high as the throne of God.

In Revelation 4:3 he depicts the throne of God as follows:

And He who was sitting was like a jasper stone and a
sardius in appearance; and there was a rainbow around
the throne, like an emerald in appearance.

In God's special providence John saw God and His throne, but he could not see the details of God's face, for the lights coming out from His face were too strong. Just like we cannot look at the shining sun because of strong light, we cannot see the image of God who is Light as long as we have spiritual darkness in us. To be able to see God's image, we have to cast off evil and have the heart of God to become a perfect light. Only those who enter into the Third Kingdom of Heaven or above can see God's image.

John's spirit went up to God's throne but he could not see the actual form of God's face. So, he said God was like a jasper stone and a sardius in appearance.

'Like jasper stone' means there are various kinds of lights being emanated from God. If you shine light on jasper, it will reflect many kinds of beautiful lights, and similarly there are many different kinds of lights coming out from God. Jasper also carries the meaning of 'purity, being free of blemish, honest, and righteous'. John the apostle described God comparing Him with a precious gemstone that people consider valuable on this earth.

'Like sardius' symbolizes that God is bright and brilliant, and He is beautiful like a flame of fire. Sardius, which is reddish in color, contains the light of the Holy Spirit who is in God. God the Father and God the Holy Spirit are one, and the light that the Holy Spirit harbors is also found in God the Father. Therefore, the colors of jasper and sardius are commonly found in all the Trinity.

The 'Rainbow' symbolizes promise (Genesis 9:12-13). God showed a rainbow as a sign of His promise that He would never punish the mankind with water after the flood of Noah. John is comparing the shape of rainbow that encircles the throne of God and the lights coming out from it with emerald. He likened the colors and lights of rainbow to the emerald within the limitations of his knowledge.

Emerald symbolizes God's firmness, boldness, and strength. In a laser show we see different lights stand out at different moments. Different colors of lights appear in a sequence, or they mingle together to create more of a grand scene. When people see these shows, each one will express the light differently. Some might just focus on a couple of special colors while others try to explain the mixed colors with an example.

The apostle John also saw the light coming out from God, the throne of God, and the lights of various colors coming out from the rainbow encircling it, and he expressed them with examples of precious stones. It is difficult to express the beauty of Heaven with examples of earthly objects. Therefore, we should not just think the lights that come out from God and His throne are like a couple of gemstones, but try to feel the beauty of those colorful lights in the inspiration of the Holy Spirit.

Partake in Divine Nature

In the fourth heaven God exists as light containing the chiming voice within the light. It is a place that has the strongest light and the most beautiful colors beyond any comparison. The mystery and clarity of the lights of the original God fills the whole space. It cannot be compared to anything on this earth in any human language. If one goes into that space, he can see the mysterious lights of God and feel the broadness of His heart.

Only a few selected persons who have cultivated the same space and dimension of heart with God's can go into that space by the permission of God. If a person who is not qualified to enter the space does enter, his spirit will be scattered away and disappear.

We come to have one heart with God if we enter into the dimension of perfect light as children of Light. Then, the things will be done as we harbor them in our hearts, and we can show unimaginable power of God. In order to do this, we have to recover the lost image of God and to have the heart of God. We can communicate with God to the extent that we cast off all forms of evil and accomplish whole spirit to become the perfect light. Once we achieve this state, we will receive anything we ask for in prayer, and we will be at a high position in the kingdom of heaven, too.

According to the extent to which we achieve holiness and have the resemblance to the heart of God, we can utilize the space of God going beyond human limits, and we can also see God's image. Moses saw the image of God for he was the meekest of all men on the face of the earth and he was faithful in all God's house. Abraham saw God who came down to this earth in physical form, for he was very close to the perfect light.

God made the plan for human cultivation to gain true children, and He filled us with everything pertaining to life and godliness with His mysterious power. Therefore, we must try to be neither useless nor unfruitful in the true knowledge of our Lord Jesus Christ. We can stand firmly on the calling and choosing of God as we in our faith supply moral excellence, and in our moral excellence, knowledge, and in our knowledge, self-control, and in our self-control, perseverance, and in our perseverance, godliness, and in our godliness, brotherly kindness, and in our brotherly kindness, love.

2 Peter 1:3-4 reads, "...*seeing that His divine power has granted to us everything pertaining to life and godliness, through the true knowledge of Him who called us by His own glory and excellence. For by these He has granted to us His precious and magnificent promises, so that by them you may become partakers of the divine nature, having escaped the corruption that is in the world by lust.*"

For us to partake in the divine nature is to accomplish perfect light that is good enough to be absorbed by the light of God. This way we can have the qualifications to enter into the space of God. It is to partake in divine nature if we accomplish the light that is similar to the perfect light of God and go forward to the space where the original God dwells. Now, what do we have to do to partake in divine nature?

First, we must cultivate a perfect heart of spirit.

We have to become one with God who is spirit, and thus we must cultivate perfect heart of spirit. If we have any form of evil, fleshly thoughts, or our own framework of thinking, we cannot partake in the divine nature. We have to cast away all kinds of evil (1 Thessalonians 5:22) and all fleshly thoughts (Romans 8:6) to have a heart of spirit.

To have a heart of spirit is to have a completely spiritual, true and sincere heart which God desires us to have. Only after having such a heart can we come to understand what God, the Lord, and the Holy Spirit really desire. Jesus came to this earth and experienced hunger, sorrow, tiredness, and pain. He practiced the Word of God and fulfilled the Law with love.

Even though He was going through so much pain having a body of a human being, He still followed the will of God. He did not quarrel or raise His voice but fulfilled the will of God completely by sacrificing Himself. Therefore, we must not give excuses saying human beings are weak. We have to partake in the divine nature by casting off all forms of sins and evil and having godly deeds and a godly heart.

What kind of heart do you have? I explained the qualifications that we must have to enter into the space of light, and with them we can check ourselves. We can check to what extent we have cast off works of the flesh, things of the flesh, and evil; and to what extent we have cultivated the kind of goodness that God desires; how much we love God from our heart and give out aroma of goodness; and to what extent we are bearing the nine fruits of the Holy Spirit and fruits of Beatitudes.

In regard to having peace, for example, if we can have peace with all people, it means we have a heart of spirit, we are close to the light of the Lord, and we are partaking in divine nature to that same extent. We can say we have a perfect heart of spirit only when we bear the fruits of the Holy Spirit, the spiritual love found in 1 Corinthians 13, the fruits of the Beatitudes, and fruits of the Light, and not just at 50% or 60%, but 100%.

Second, we must pray with the inspiration of the Holy Spirit.

God does not want aroma of prayer that is done out of sense of duty. He wants us to pray earnestly to cultivate the heart of God. People might pray for the same length of time but the aroma of heart is different from person to person. Some are satisfied just by the fact that they filled up the amount of daily prayer while others do not even realize the time passing when they pray, for they feel so happy praying before God to change themselves with their love for Him.

We are supposed to show works of the spiritual realm in this physical world. To do so we have to receive strength and power from God who dwells in spiritual space. Therefore, our prayers must not be offered just with a sense of duty. God wants us to pray with all our heart because we love Him.

To receive power from God, we have to offer spiritual prayers that can penetrate through the physical space and open the space of spirit. To do this we should not pray as we see fit or while preoccupied with idle thoughts. Such prayers cannot penetrate physical space. They will only be wasted. God cannot be moved by such prayers. If your children stubbornly ask you to give them only what they want out of their greed, what would you feel as parents? You would probably be disappointed.

1 Corinthians 2:10 says, *"For to us God revealed them through the Spirit; for the Spirit searches all things, even the depths of God."* We have to pray by the inspiration of the Holy Spirit who is in our heart. Then, we will be able to pray for the things that are proper according to the will of God, and we will understand what to do, too. We will be able to open the gate of spiritual space and have communication with God who is in spiritual dimension for we will be united with the Holy Spirit in us.

Third, we must love and accept everyone with virtuous generosity.

The heart of spirit that resembles heart of God already contains love and generosity, but I am putting an emphasis on love and generosity once again. It is because we must be able to love everyone around us because we love God, and we must have broad heart and generosity to be able to accept everybody. We should be full of love and generosity and take care of everyone around us who is having a hard time or who is growing weary. The heart of God is broad beyond measure, but He is so delicate and caring that He cares for orphans and widows, and the situations of the neglected.

When we care for even small things with love and edify others with our generosity, it is to partake in the divine nature. We should realize ourselves and change through God's Word to partake in the divine nature.

When we have a complete heart of light and partake in the divine nature, as I have previously explained, we can go into the space of light and the space of God. If we go into the space of God, we will be able to see the special light of that space. We will also feel the heart of God that is so broad and big. Furthermore, even though our physical body is in the physical space, we will use the space of God that we possess in our heart to manifest such amazing things that are beyond human understanding.

1 John 1:5 says, *"This is the message we have heard from Him and announce to you, that God is Light, and in Him there is no darkness at all."* If we dwell in the perfect light of God, it means we have one heart with God, and anything we harbor in heart will be realized, and we will perform great power that men cannot imagine.

I pray in the name of the Lord that you will all have such qualifications so that you will enjoy on this earth all the blessings that Abraham enjoyed, and go into the most glorious positions in Heaven, an eternal space of light.

The Author
Dr. Jaerock Lee

Dr. Jaerock Lee was born in Muan, Jeonnam Province, Republic of Korea, in 1943. In his twenties, Dr. Lee suffered from a variety of incurable diseases for seven years and awaited death with no hope for recovery. One day in the spring of 1974, however, he was led to a church by his sister and when he knelt down to pray, the living God immediately healed him of all his diseases.

From the moment Dr. Lee met the living God through that wonderful experience, he has loved God with all his heart and sincerity, and in 1978 he was called to be a servant of God. He prayed fervently with countless fasting prayers so that he could clearly understand the will of God, wholly accomplish it and obey the Word of God. In 1982, he founded Manmin Central Church in Seoul, Korea, and countless works of God, including miraculous healings, signs and wonders, have been taking place at his church.

In 1986, Dr. Lee was ordained as a pastor at the Annual Assembly of Jesus' Sungkyul Church of Korea, and four years later in 1990, his sermons began to be broadcast in Australia, Russia, the Philippines, and many more through the Far East Broadcasting Company, the Asia Broadcast Station, and the Washington Christian Radio System.

Three years later in 1993, Manmin Central Church was selected as one of the "World's Top 50 Churches" by the Christian World magazine (US) and he received an Honorary Doctorate of Divinity from Christian Faith College, Florida, USA, and in 1996 a Ph. D. in Ministry from Kingsway Theological Seminary, Iowa, USA.

Since 1993, Dr. Lee has been spearheading world evangelization through many overseas crusades in Tanzania, Argentina, L.A., Baltimore City, Hawaii, and New York City of the USA, Uganda, Japan, Pakistan, Kenya, the Philippines, Honduras, India, Russia, Germany, Peru, Democratic Republic of the Congo, Israel and Estonia.

In 2002 he was called a "worldwide revivalist" by major Christian newspapers in Korea for his powerful ministries in various overseas crusades. Especially, his 'New York Crusade 2006' held in Madison Square Garden, the most world-famous arena, was broadcast to 220 nations, and in his 'Israel United Crusade 2009' held in International Convention Center in Jerusalem he boldly proclaimed Jesus Christ is the Messiah and Savior. His sermon is brodacst to 176 nations via satellites including GCN TV and he was listed as one of the Top 10 Most Influential Christian Leaders of 2009 and 2010 by the Russian popular Christian magazine *In Victory* and new agency *Christian Telegraph* for his powerful TV broadcasting ministry and overseas church-pastoring ministry.

As of March of 2013, Manmin Central Church has a congregation of more than 120,000 members. There are 10,000 branch churches throughout the globe including 57 domestic branch churches, and so far more than 129 missionaries have been commissioned to 23 countries, including the United States, Russia, Germany, Canada, Japan, China, France, India, Kenya, and many more.

As of the date of this publishing, Dr. Lee has written 84 books, including bestsellers *Tasting Eternal Life before Death, My Life My Faith I & II, The Message of the Cross, The Measure of Faith, Heaven I & II, Hell,* and *The Power of God.* His works have been translated into more than 75 languages.

His Christian columns appear on *The Hankook Ilbo, The JoongAng Daily, The Chosun Ilbo, The Dong-A Ilbo, The Munhwa Ilbo, The Seoul Shinmun, The Kyunghyang Shinmun, The Korea Economic Daily, The Korea Herald, The Sisa News,* and *The Christian Press.*

Dr. Lee is currently leader of many missionary organizations and associations: including Chairman, The United Holiness Church of Jesus Christ; President, Manmin World Mission; Permanent President, The World Christianity Revival Mission Association; Founder & Board Chairman, Global Christian Network (GCN); Founder & Board Chairman, World Christian Doctors Network (WCDN); and Founder & Board Chairman, Manmin International Seminary (MIS).

Heaven I & II

A detailed sketch of the gorgeous living environment the heavenly citizens enjoy and beautiful description of different levels of heavenly kingdoms.

The Message of the Cross

A powerful awakening message for all the people who are spiritually asleep! In this book you will find the reason Jesus is the only Savior and the true love of God.

Hell

An earnest message to all mankind from God, who wishes not even one soul to fall into the depths of Hell! You will discover the never-before-revealed account of the cruel reality of the Lower Grave and Hell.

Spirit, Soul, and Body I

A guidebook that gives the reader spiritual understanding of spirit, soul, and body, and helps him find what kind of 'self' he has made so that he can gain the power to defeat darkness and become a person of spirit.

The Measure of Faith

What kind of a dwelling place, crown and reward are prepared for you in Heaven? This book provides with wisdom and guidance for you to measure your faith and cultivate the best and most mature faith.

Awaken, Israel

Why has God kept His eyes on Israel from the beginning of the world to this day? What kind of His providence has been prepared for Israel in the last days, who await the Messiah?

My Life My Faith I & II

Dr. Jaerock Lee's autobiography provides the most fragrant spiritual aroma for the readers, through his life extracted from the love of God blossomed in midst of the dark waves, cold yoke and the deepest despair.

Seven Churches

The letter to the seven churches of the Lord in the book of Revelation is for all the churches that have existed up until now. It is like a signpost for them and a summary of all the words of God in both Old and New Testaments.